Digital Entrepreneurship and Disruptive Innovation

A new generation of entrepreneurs are leveraging artificial intelligence, data analytics, the Internet of Things (IoT) and other revolutionary technologies for greater social and environmental good. These digital entrepreneurs are developing disruptive solutions to the most pressing sustainability challenges of our time. Yet, behind every case of a successful digital entrepreneur is a wider network of governments, startup incubators and accelerators, incumbent firms, universities and other actors that form a regional entrepreneurial ecosystem.

Through in-depth case studies, this book explores how digital entrepreneurs across various geographic regions use disruptive innovation within their regional entrepreneurial ecosystems to leverage digital technologies that create and develop novel business solutions crucial to meeting the United Nations' Sustainable Development Goals. Exploring the perspectives of digital entrepreneurs themselves, each chapter in this book presents a case study that reveals how cultural differences and local socio-economic factors enable digital entrepreneurship driven by disruptive innovation.

This book offers insights and recommendations through the stories of digital entrepreneurs across geographic regions for researchers, graduate students, practitioners and public- and private-sector leaders on harnessing the combined power of disruptive innovation and regional entrepreneurial ecosystems to fuel regional economic growth and sustainable development.

Jordi Diaz, DBA, is the Dean of EADA Business School Barcelona and the Director of the Executive Academy of the European Foundation for Management Development (EFMD Global). Dr. Diaz holds an

Executive Doctorate of Business Administration (EDBA) from Ecole des Ponts ParisTech Business School (France), a Master's degree in Human Resources Management from EADA Business School, and professional certificates from Harvard Business School.

Daphne Halkias, PhD, is the Dean of Doctoral Programs at EIM - European Institute of Management, Distinguished Research Fellow at the Center for Policy and Competitiveness at Ecole des Ponts ParisTech Business School, and Fellow at the Institute of Coaching at McLean Hospital, a Harvard Medical School affiliate. She is a research affiliate at the Cornell Center for the Social Sciences, Cornell University, and CEO and Founder of Executive Coaching Consultants.

Tatiana Harkiolakis, MSc, is a DBA candidate at ISC Paris Business School and a research fellow at the Center for Policy and Competitiveness at Ecole des Ponts ParisTech Business School. She is also the Director of Communications at Executive Coaching Consultants and holds an MSc in Communications and Media from the London School of Economics and Political Science.

Routledge Focus on Business and Management

The fields of business and management have grown exponentially as areas of research and education. This growth presents challenges for readers trying to keep up with the latest important insights. *Routledge Focus on Business and Management* presents small books on big topics and how they intersect with the world of business research.

Individually, each title in the series provides coverage of a key academic topic, whilst collectively, the series forms a comprehensive collection across the business disciplines.

Grassroots Social Innovation
The Role of Collaboration and Experiential Learning
Karolina Osterczuk

Leadership in the Pharmaceutical Industry
From Theory to Practice
Nataliia Aliekperova

Retiring in a New Age
Life after Paid Work
Russell D. Lansbury and Marian Baird

Digital Entrepreneurship and Disruptive Innovation
Intersections of Regional Development, Innovation Systems, and Sustainability
Jordi Diaz, Daphne Halkias and Tatiana Harkiolakis

For more information about this series, please visit: www.routledge.com/Routledge-Focus-on-Business-and-Management/book-series/FBM

Digital Entrepreneurship and Disruptive Innovation

Intersections of Regional Development, Innovation Systems, and Sustainability

Jordi Diaz, Daphne Halkias and Tatiana Harkiolakis

Routledge
Taylor & Francis Group
NEW YORK AND LONDON

First published 2026
by Routledge
605 Third Avenue, New York, NY 10158

and by Routledge
4 Park Square, Milton Park, Abingdon, Oxon, OX14 4RN

Routledge is an imprint of the Taylor & Francis Group, an informa business

ISBN: 978-1-041-01717-2 (hbk)
ISBN: 978-1-041-01721-9 (pbk)
ISBN: 978-1-003-61610-8 (ebk)

DOI: 10.4324/9781003616108

Typeset in Times New Roman
by Newgen Publishing UK

Contents

Author Biographies *ix*
Contributor Biographies *xi*

1 Introduction: Digital Entrepreneurship and Disruptive Innovation—How Regional Ecosystems Shape the Future of Business 1
TATIANA HARKIOLAKIS

2 Peru: SaludAbierta: An E-Healthcare Service Innovation Case Study for Enhanced Healthcare Access in Peru 6
JORDI DIAZ, DAPHNE HALKIAS AND TATIANA HARKIOLAKIS

3 United Arab Emirates: Disrupting Food Waste in the UAE—The Case of The Waste Lab 18
JORDI DIAZ, DAPHNE HALKIAS AND TATIANA HARKIOLAKIS

4 Spain: Challenging Established Norms—Wine in a Can, Inc. and Disruptive Innovation in the Wine Industry 31
JORDI DIAZ, DAPHNE HALKIAS AND TATIANA HARKIOLAKIS

5 India: AI in Diagnostics and Healthcare Accessibility—The Disruptive Model of Larkai Healthcare 39
JORDI DIAZ, DAPHNE HALKIAS AND TATIANA HARKIOLAKIS

6 Ivory Coast: Djamo—Bridging the Financial Divide in Francophone Africa 50
JORDI DIAZ, RAY SANDERS MUHAMMAD AND TATIANA HARKIOLAKIS

7 Cyprus: Transforming the Workspace Culture in Cyprus—The Journey of MyOffice Cyprus 69
MARCOS KOMODROMOS AND MARIOS VASSILIOU

8 Jordan: Ethnic Fashion and Sustainability in the MENA Region —The Case of Sanaa Mohammad in Jordan 81
TATIANA HARKIOLAKIS, BAKER AHMAD ALSERHAN AND RUBA NIZAR QAHOUSH

Index *101*

Author Biographies

Jordi Diaz, DBA, is the Dean of EADA Business School Barcelona and the Director of the Executive Academy of the European Foundation for Management Development (EFMD Global). Dr. Diaz holds an Executive Doctorate of Business Administration (EDBA) from Ecole des Ponts ParisTech Business School (France), a Master's degree in Human Resources Management from EADA Business School and professional certificates from Harvard Business School. Dr. Diaz serves on advisory boards at several business schools and is the Editor of the *International Journal of Environment, Workplace and Employment*. He co-authored the bestselling management education book *The Innovative Management Education Ecosystem*. Dr. Diaz's community service memberships include Business Fights Poverty and the Excellence in Sustainability Club in Spain.

Daphne Halkias, PhD, is the Dean of Doctoral Programs at EIM - European Institute of Management, Distinguished Research Fellow at the Center for Policy and Competitiveness at Ecole des Ponts ParisTech Business School, and Fellow at the Institute of Coaching at McLean Hospital, a Harvard Medical School affiliate. She is a research affiliate at the Cornell Center for the Social Sciences, Cornell University, and CEO and Founder of Executive Coaching Consultants. Dr. Halkias is a distinguished scholar with over 150 peer-reviewed scientific papers and has co-authored several best-selling academic books, including the recent *The Innovative Business School* and *The Multiple Case Study Design* with Prof Dr. Michael Neubert. She is Editor-in-Chief of three academic journals and sits on various editorial and advisory boards. Dr. Halkias' community service memberships include Business Fights Poverty.

Tatiana Harkiolakis, MSc, is a DBA candidate at ISC Paris Business School and a research fellow at the Center for Policy and Competitiveness at Ecole des Ponts ParisTech Business School. She is also the Director of Communications at Executive Coaching Consultants and holds an MSc in Communications and Media from the London School of Economics and Political Science. Ms Harkiolakis is a published journalist and academic researcher with several publications in the areas of entrepreneurship, emerging digital technologies, and media and communications.

Contributor Biographies

Baker Ahmad Alserhan is Professor of Business Administration at Princess Sumaya University in Amman, Jordan.

Marcos Komodromos is Professor of Marketing and Communications at the University of Nicosia in Nicosia, Cyprus, in the Communications Department, and a chartered PR practitioner at the Chartered Institute of Public Relations (CIPR) in Great Britain.

Ray Sanders Muhammad is Professor of Accounting and Business at Georgia State University Perimeter College in Alpharetta, Georgia, USA, and Faculty at University of Maryland Global University in the United States. In addition to his career in academia, Dr. Sanders Muhammad is an entrepreneur.

Ruba Nizar Qahoush is a Master's student of Business Entrepreneurship at Princess Sumaya University in Amman, Jordan.

Marios Vassiliou is an associate lecturer in marketing and communications at the University of Central Lancashire, in Larnaca, Cyprus.

1 Introduction

Digital Entrepreneurship and Disruptive Innovation: How Regional Ecosystems Shape the Future of Business

Tatiana Harkiolakis

Regional entrepreneurial ecosystems driven by disruptive innovation may play a crucial role in supporting digital entrepreneurs to create and disseminate new products and services along with new ideas about the role of other social actors with whom they interact, generating a collective value that exceeds the sum of individual contributions (Lechner et al., 2022). Actors within these regional ecosystems may include individual entrepreneurs, local firms, governments, startup incubators and accelerators, research labs and other public, private and third-sector entities (Bakry et al., 2022; Lechner et al., 2022). Digitalization across geographic regions and new interconnected open tools offer digital entrepreneurs opportunities for innovative methods of working and collaborating on development projects across regions, countries and continents (Takala & Tukiainen, 2022). However, little is known about how digital entrepreneurs across various geographic regions use disruptive innovation within their regional entrepreneurial ecosystems to leverage digital technologies that create and develop novel business solutions crucial to meeting the United Nations' Sustainable Development Goals (Xu et al., 2022).

Innovation is a key driver of economic growth and firm performance, especially in regional ecosystems (Araki et al., 2024). As an extension, innovative digital entrepreneurship is becoming a crucial component of regional ecosystems. Innovation is seen as creating new markets and boosting demand, which spurs job creation and higher incomes, and improving productivity, which leads to increased competitiveness and the development of new sectors and industries (Si et al., 2023). New business models and ecosystems are enabled by the

DOI: 10.4324/9781003616108-1

rise of digital technologies, which allow entrepreneurs to drive disruptive innovation (Halkias et al., 2023).

Previous research indicated that incumbents' business models can be severely disrupted by the emergence of new entrants in an ecosystem who capture more value than incumbents (Cozzolino & Geiger, 2024). However, the relationship between disruptive innovation and ecosystems remains understudied, calling for more research on how multiple actors in an ecosystem create and capture value in the context of disruptive innovation (Baldwin et al., 2024). Additionally, existing research on ecosystems tends to focus on the role of firms as actors in ecosystems and less on the role of individuals as actors (Altman et al., 2023). Regional entrepreneurship also lacks a robust empirical and theoretical connection to innovation and ecosystems, even though regional entrepreneurship ecosystems play a crucial role in economic growth and are equally capable of delivering disruptive innovations (Baldwin et al., 2024; Si et al., 2023).

Regional ecosystems include individuals and organizations such as universities, public agencies and private firms, all centered in a specific geographical region (Stam & Spigel, 2018). Innovative ecosystems involve value being created through products or processes sold in a market for a price, whereas in entrepreneurial ecosystems, value is created through productive entrepreneurial activities (Baldwin et al., 2024). In an extension of regional and innovative ecosystems, disruptive innovation ecosystems have been conceptualized as ecosystems capable of delivering disruptive innovations (Nthubu et al., 2019). Disruptive innovation, a process by which entrants' niche products, services and business models grow to overtake those of incumbents, plays a particular role in spurring regional economic growth by stimulating competitiveness and sustainable company growth (Si et al., 2023). Despite this role, little research has been done that examines disruptive innovation from a regional ecosystem lens (Halkias et al., 2023).

Disruptive innovation ecosystems foster entrepreneurial activities, providing a supportive environment for innovative and sustainable business models (Nthubu et al., 2021). Digital sustainable entrepreneurship is at the forefront of the evolving business landscape, especially within disruptive innovation ecosystems, integrating sustainability principles into the digital and technological realms and creating new opportunities for value creation and environmental stewardship (Gregori & Holzmann, 2020). Emerging digital technologies are having a resounding effect on economic and social life. A new generation of entrepreneurs is leveraging artificial intelligence, data analytics, the Internet of Things (IoT) and other revolutionary technologies for greater social and environmental good. These digital entrepreneurs are developing disruptive solutions to our time's most pressing sustainability challenges (Holzmann & Gregori, 2023).

Understanding and engaging with these trends in the immediate and long term will be crucial for entrepreneurs, investors and policymakers looking to foster innovation that drives economic growth and addresses critical environmental and social challenges (Xu et al., 2022). The nexus of disruptive innovation, regional ecosystems and digital sustainable entrepreneurship is rich and multifaceted (Baldwin et al., 2024). It involves understanding how emerging technologies and innovative business models transform industries in ways that contribute to sustainability, particularly in developing and developed economies challenged over the last two decades by a volatile macroeconomic outlook (Balta et al., 2023).

Cultural differences across the various geographic regions in developing and developed markets must be seen as an essential element of such case studies to clarify further how local socioeconomic factors enable digital entrepreneurship driven by disruptive innovation, an essential driver of economic development in today's global marketplace (Schrijvers et al., 2024). Behind every case of a successful digital entrepreneur is a broader network of governments, startup incubators and accelerators, incumbent firms, universities and other actors that form a regional entrepreneurial ecosystem. Nevertheless, little is known about regional disruptive innovation ecosystems and the role of individuals as value-creating actors in these ecosystems. Through in-depth case studies, this book explores how digital entrepreneurs across various geographic regions use disruptive innovation within their regional entrepreneurial ecosystems to leverage digital technologies that create and develop novel business solutions.

Each chapter in this book presents an entrepreneur's story that reveals how cultural differences and local socioeconomic factors enable business growth driven by disruptive innovation. We hope this collection of cross-national case studies offers insights and recommendations across geographic regions for researchers, graduate students, practitioners and public- and private-sector leaders on harnessing the combined power of disruptive innovation and regional entrepreneurial ecosystems to fuel regional economic growth and sustainable development.

References

Altman, E. J., Kiron, D., Schwartz, J., & Jones, R. (2023). *Workforce ecosystems: reaching strategic goals with people, partners, and technologies*. MIT Press.

Araki, M. E., Bennett, D. L., & Wagner, G. A. (2024). Regional innovation networks & high-growth entrepreneurship. *Research Policy*, *53*(1), Article 104900. https://doi.org/10.1016/j.respol.2023.104900

Bakry, D. S., Daim, T., Dabic, M., & Yesilada, B. (2022). An evaluation of the effectiveness of innovation ecosystems in facilitating the adoption of sustainable entrepreneurship. *Journal of Small Business Management*, *62*(2), 763–789. https://doi.org/10.1080/00472778.2022.2088775

Baldwin, C. Y., Bogers, M. L., Kapoor, R., & West, J. (2024). Focusing the ecosystem lens on innovation studies. *Research Policy*, *53*(3), Article 104949. https://doi.org/10.1016/j.respol.2023.104949

Balta, M., Spanaki, K., Papadopoulos, T., & Ravishankar, M. N. (2023). Understanding the use of digital technologies in entrepreneurial start-up settings and growth-oriented firms [Editorial]. *International Journal of Information Management*, *69*, Article 102616. https://doi.org/10.1016/j.ijinfomgt.2022.102616

Cozzolino, A. & Geiger, S. (2024). Ecosystem disruption and regulatory positioning: Entry strategies of digital health startup orchestrators and complementors. *Research Policy*, *53*(2), Article 104913. https://doi.org/10.1016/j.respol.2023.104913

Gregori, P. & Holzmann, P. (2020). Digital sustainable entrepreneurship: A business model perspective on embedding digital technologies for social and environmental value creation. *Journal of Cleaner Production*, *272*, Article 122817. https://doi.org/10.1016/j.jclepro.2020.122817

Halkias, D., Esposito, M., Harkiolakis, T., Diaz, J., & Ikpogu, N. M. (2023). Digital entrepreneurship and disruptive innovation in the Greek maritime industry: The case of Harbor Lab. In V. Ramadani, S. Kjosev, & B. S. Sergi (Eds.), *Entrepreneurship development in the Balkans: Perspective from diverse contexts* (pp. 131–150). Emerald Publishing Limited.

Holzmann, P. & Gregori, P. (2023). The promise of digital technologies for sustainable entrepreneurship: A systematic literature review and research agenda. *International Journal of Information Management*, *68*, Article 102593. https://doi.org/10.1016/j.ijinfomgt.2022.102593

Lechner, C., Delanoë-Gueguen, S., & Gueguen, G. (2022). Entrepreneurial ecosystems and actor legitimacy. *International Journal of Entrepreneurial Behavior & Research*, *28*(9), 466–491. https://doi.org/10.1108/IJEBR-03-2020-0165

Nthubu, B., Richards, D., & Cruickshank, L. (2019). Disruptive innovation ecosystems: Reconceptualising innovation ecosystems. In E. Bohemia, G. Gemser, N. Fain, C. de Bont, & R. Assoreira Almendra (Eds.), *Conference proceedings of the Academy for Design Innovation Management: Research perspectives in the era of transformations* (pp. 629–644). Academy for Design Innovation Management. www.aacademica.org/del.giorgio.solfa/219

Nthubu, B., Richards, D., & Cruickshank, L. (2021). Designing conditions for disruptive innovation ecosystems. In G. Bruyns & H. Wei (Eds.), *With design: Reinventing design modes – Proceedings of the 9th Congress of the International Association of Societies of Design Research (IASDR 2021)* (pp. 1705–1730). Springer Singapore. https://doi.org/10.1007/978-981-19-4472-7_111

Schrijvers, M., Stam, E., & Bosma, N. (2024). Figuring it out: Configurations of high-performing entrepreneurial ecosystems in Europe. *Regional Studies, 58*(5), 1096–1110. https://doi.org/10.1080/00343404.2023.2226727

Si, S., Hall, J., Suddaby, R., Ahlstrom, D., & Wei, J. (2023). Technology, entrepreneurship, innovation and social change in digital economics. *Technovation, 119*, Article 102484. https://doi.org/10.1016/j.technovation.2022.102484

Stam, E. & Spigel, B. (2018). Entrepreneurial ecosystems. In R. Blackburn, D. De Clercq, & J. Heinonen (Eds.), *Sage handbook of entrepreneurship and small business* (pp. 407–422). Sage. https://doi.org/10.4135/9781473984080.n21

Takala, M. & Tukiainen, T. (2022). Regional innovation ecosystems fostering sustainable development. In V. Salminen (Ed.), *Human factors, business management and society: Proceedings of the 13th International Conference on Applied Human Factors and Ergonomics (AHFE 2022)* (Vol. 56, pp. 17–24). AHFE International.

Xu, G., Hou, G., & Zhang, J. (2022). Digital sustainable entrepreneurship: A digital capability perspective through digital innovation orientation for social and environmental value creation. *Sustainability, 14*(18), Article 11222. https://doi.org/10.3390/su141811222

2 Peru: SaludAbierta

An E-Healthcare Service Innovation Case Study for Enhanced Healthcare Access in Peru

Jordi Diaz, Daphne Halkias and Tatiana Harkiolakis

After a frantic first six months as CEO of SaludAbierta—a newly created digital venture of the Salud Group—Ana Marin said to herself that the real opportunity for the company lay not in digitizing its current services but in giving access—at a scale—to the 24 million people that today had no access to medical treatment and a healthcare system regularly. "There should be a way to turn this challenge into a real business opportunity for the company and the people of my country". In the middle of her brainstorming, Ana received a message from her Group's CEO fixing a meeting to know her plans for SaludAbierta, after she stabilized the digital transition of the new division of the Salud Group in Peru.

The Protagonist's Dilemma

Ana Marin spent more than ten years at multinational corporations operating in the fast-moving consumer goods (FMCG) industry. She worked for brand names such as Alicorp, Coca-Cola, Nestle and PepsiCo, developing her expertise in marketing and communications. While having a very successful initial corporate career, Ana felt something was missing and decided to enroll in an International MBA at EADA Business School in Barcelona to find it. This opportunity, based far from her home country and enabling her to be surrounded by colleagues from around the world, allowed her to refine her business skills, a crucial need for business leaders (Diaz & Halkias, 2021) and, most importantly, to reflect on her bigger goals in life. Beyond career ambitions, what did she want to achieve as her legacy?

DOI: 10.4324/9781003616108-2

Back in Peru from her MBA studies, she was offered a three-month internship with Amazon, where she discovered one of her main passions, technology. Then she was hired as the Country Marketing Director by Barcelona-based Unicorn Glovo. Two years later, Glovo's operation in Peru was sold to PedidosYa, another Unicorn in the delivery service industry, where she stayed another six months. Although working for these hyper-growing companies was exciting and enriching, her fundamental question about her legacy was not resolved.

Ana, the daughter of medical doctors, received a call in July 2021 that started to connect all the dots. Ana was approached to join private healthcare provider the Salud Group as the Venture CEO for e-pharmacy SaludAbierta. After her experience in both technology startups and established multinationals, her move to healthcare technology made her the ideal candidate to lead the recently launched (January 2021) SaludAbierta. The project aimed to be a strategic building block of the Salud Group's vision of accessible healthcare for millions of users, through a convenient set of e-pharmacy services.

While it was conceived as the e-pharmacy of the group, in previous conversations with the Salud Group Steering Committee, Ana was able to grasp a genuine interest in turning the new venture into something else with much greater outreach. One slide still resonated in Ana's mind during the interview with Manuel Casanova, the Group's CEO.

However, Ana knew that the only way to convince the 75% of Peruvians who were non-consumers of the healthcare industry would be to break the wealth barrier by decreasing the prices drastically through generic medicines. This, of course, would have direct implications for the profit formula: it required a significant drop in gross margins and a radical reduction in many cost structure elements. She thought, however, that she could still make a profit by increasing the sales volume dramatically within a large-sized target base of consumers.

Ana wondered if generating revenue through a monthly subscription model was possible. Customers could have their medicines, complementary products and services at their fingertips for a monthly fee. However, this would require an even more significant fundamental shift in all major components of the profit formula: revenue stream (pricing, staging of payments and how to think about volume), cost structure (including added sales development costs), supporting margins and transaction fulfillment speed.

For the next six months, Ana defined the following key priorities:

Resources

- Hiring innovative, talented people to ensure growth and improve user experience and cost reduction while achieving product market-fit.

Processes

- Mastering the process of continuously forming new hypotheses and testing new ideas as the company's core innovation mindset.
- Achieving integration and synergies with the rest of the Salud Group ecosystem.
    - i. Integration of SaludAbierta with the customer journeys of other Salud Group units.
    - ii. Leverage the Salud Group's (Cancersalud) customer bases for customer acquisition.
    - iii. Take advantage of the purchasing power in medicines of the Salud Group service.

Profit Formula

- Spotlighting key segments: acute and chronic patients—including cancer—especially in current non-consumers of the healthcare industry.

The Business/Social Opportunity for the Salud Group

The conglomerate offered its services and products to the top 25% of the economic pyramid. However, what about the remaining 75% of Peruvians, who were non-consumers of the healthcare industry? What about all the remaining Peruvians who do not have access to non-communicable disease treatment? Why weren't they considered consumers?

The first and the most apparent reason was affordability. Essential patient treatment costs approximately ten soles daily, which 90% of the urban poor in Peru, who earn just S/. 25 or less a day, cannot afford. Nevertheless, affordability was not the only reason. Accessibility was also an issue for many people. Not all urban and rural areas had enough hospitals, doctors, trained personnel or medicines.

Today, out of the 33 million inhabitants in Peru, only 9 million have the purchasing power to buy corporations' goods and services. There were 24 million non-consumers who represented the single most significant growth opportunity for the Salud Group, and most of these non-consumers were in emerging markets; this was perhaps the single most significant opportunity in the Salud Group's history.

The Current Challenge/Business Problem/Challenge Questions

The present business goal for SaludAbierta is to offer access to pharmacy services or other healthcare services (including education, access to health teams, information and health monitoring through telemedicine services and across emerging markets). Ana had one week to prepare for the Salud Group Steering Committee meeting and map out a business plan to meet SaludAbierta's telemedicine business goal. Working for six months at leading SaludAbierta gave her the clarity to see the ample opportunity to turn Peruvian non-patients into patients within an e-healthcare system. She knew the Steering Committee would not accept a simple idea but a detailed plan, to start considering her idea.

While preparing for the meeting, the following questions started to circle in her mind:

- How could we bring healthcare to every corner of the country?
- How does this new business compare to the current segment served by Salud Group?
- Addressing the low-end segment of the market, how should the new business be organized for success? What would be the best governance for SaludAbierta's new low-end segment?
- Should the Salud Group continue to serve current clients (Groups A/B) and incorporate the new segments (Groups C to E) under the same "SaludAbierta" name & structure, or create a separate business unit? What were the risks and opportunities of operating both options inside or outside the company's firm?
- What could be the primary "resistance" by the Steering Committee?

Background

More than 183,000 lives and 35 billion Peruvian soles (US$ 9 billion) could be saved over the next 15 years by implementing a set of policies to reduce tobacco, alcohol and salt use and by scaling up clinical interventions to control cardiovascular disease and diabetes, as well as increasing access to treatment for depression, anxiety and psychiatric conditions.

> A study carried out by the Pan American Health Organization (PAHO) and the United Nations Development Program (UNDP) in collaboration with the Ministry of Health of Peru and supported by the Research Triangle Institute (RTI)[1] showed that for every Peruvian sol invested in the joint implementation of this package of measures, 2.2 soles could be expected in return over 15 years through averted economic productivity losses combined with lower health expenditure in a healthier population. Increased productivity would contribute to economic expansion, generating more than a quarter of a percentage point (0.28%) of GDP growth in 15 years.

Hypertension and diabetes, also known as non-communicable diseases, kill 1.5 million people yearly.[2] Moreover, deaths from these diseases disproportionately occur in low- and middle-income countries, where governments and health systems have been weakened by centuries of injustice, including corruption. Diabetes, hypertension and other chronic diseases, such as asthma and heart disease, put patients at increased risk of severe illness from COVID-19.

Approximately one person in four in Latin America is at increased risk of a poor outcome if they become ill with COVID-19 due to underlying NCDs.[3] One of the most concerning aspects of the current pandemic is its disproportionate impact on people suffering from NCDs such as cardiovascular diseases, diabetes, cancer and chronic respiratory diseases, as well as obesity. Detecting these diseases early and providing treatment and medication were critical for patients' health and well-being, especially in countries like Peru, in impoverished communities on the outskirts of Lima where thousands lacked access to quality care.

Peru and Access to Healthcare

In South America's central and western areas, Peru has a surface area of 1,285,215 km^2. It is divided into 25 regions and Metropolitan Lima, the capital city, 195 provinces and 1,834 municipalities. In 2020, the country's population was 32.9 mh.[4] Of that total, 30% were under

15 years old, 8.6% were more than 60 years old and 74.0% lived in urban areas. Between 2006 and 2020, Peru's economy grew at an annual rate above 2.5%, except in 2020, due to COVID-19. Although poverty was substantially reduced, vast inequalities persisted in income distribution. Despite the positive economic performance, with good macroeconomic results, a significant concentration of income persisted. In 2020, the income of the wealthiest quintile was 12.5 times greater than that of the poorest quintile, accounting for 52.6% of national income, compared with 4.2% for the poorest quintile.

The health situation had improved; however, access to essential services such as drinking water and sewerage had increased, particularly in rural areas. Despite improvements in the health situation, there were significant challenges for public health, such as reducing the burden of communicable diseases by eliminating mother-to-child transmission and preventing and controlling non-communicable chronic diseases—nationwide access to quality health services needed to be increased, and decentralization and universal insurance were necessary. Furthermore, strengthening the steering role of the Ministry of Health and the management of the Regional Health Bureaus were needed to improve healthcare access for those who could not even afford primary healthcare.

Achieving healthcare access for an impoverished population will require better coordination among the health services, a higher public budget, improved mechanisms for referring patients and expanded activities for promotion and prevention. It would also be necessary to strengthen the health information system to monitor and evaluate health actions and measure their impact on population health, particularly that of the poorer and excluded groups. Finally, training needed to be intensified, along with the exchange of information among the different sectors that delivered health services.

Despite globalization and the technological advancements in healthcare globally, access in Peru to healthcare and other basic needs remained a fundamental problem for the economically underprivileged. At the same time, this situation represented an opportunity for those with the willpower and resources to provide a unique solution for the underserved population.

The Salud Group

The Salud Group was part of the Institute of Salud (IoS). The conglomerate comprises seven clinics, two clinical laboratories, and a specialty school focused on health sciences. Within the IoS, the Salud Group had most of the private sector patient population, including around 800,000 patients in a highly competitive market.

Since its inception in 2008, its strategy has focused on bringing health and well-being to its members and patients. The Salud Group's medical team formed the leading institution in preventing, detecting and treating cancer in Peru. Constant renewal and reinvention activities allowed the Salud Group to provide its patients with the best services and experiences. A current focus, accelerated by the pandemic, was the shift into the digital world. A strong portfolio of digital products and partnerships had been put in place to aid in incubating and scaling digital solutions.

The strategically deployed digital healthcare platforms included Clinica Global, SaludAbierta and SaludAplica. These platforms serve patients in Chile, Colombia, Mexico and Peru, with the potential to make healthcare more accessible and convenient. In addition, health-tech partnerships expanded the Salud Group's reach into the Colombian and US markets. Implementing these technologies positioned the Salud Group as a leading healthcare provider, poised to revolutionize the industry.

SaludAbierta

SaludAbierta was conceived as a strategic building block and had two critical roles for the Salud Group's vision as its convenient e-pharmacy: i) to be an important source of customers for the Salud Group and ii) to be a critical service as a main entry point to the Salud Group ecosystem for non-consumers.

To SaludAbierta, the essential resources were its people and culture (agile, candid and data-driven), and the key processes were naturally people-related (training, development) and had to do with continuous A/B testing, mainly consisting of forming hypotheses and testing new ideas. This last process became critical to survival when transformational growth was needed to defend against disruptive rivals.

SaludAbierta was launched in Peru in February 2021 as a strategic building block of the Salud Group's vision and ecosystem to access millions of users through a convenient e-pharmacy.

- Portfolio with +4k SKUs includes the most requested products between consumption and pharmacy.

- Twelve dark stores guarantee rapid distribution throughout the city of Lima.
- A promise of delivery in 75 minutes/24x7 to 30 districts of Lima.
- Digital experience with a four-step purchase process.
- The online platform guarantees 99% product availability.

Pharmacies have the potential to become health management centers and deliver treatment to help keep patients healthy at home and out of the hospital, rather than simply being considered medication fulfillment centers. SaludAbierta provides more personalized healthcare, advice, guidance and a more comprehensive array of services. It is a meaningful touchpoint for building trust and strong relationships with current and potential customers. SaludAbierta allows customers to complete an entire pharmacy transaction on their desktop or mobile device. Customers can order from their phones whenever, wherever.

The Salud Group healthcare ecosystem is the only one that connects a nationwide network of doctors with a pharmacy to deliver personalized treatment directly to your door. This ecosystem enables physicians, nurses and pharmacists in the Salud Group's clinics and health centers to seamlessly track a patient journey and facilitate frictionless care coordination to provide high-quality care from diagnosis to medication delivery to ongoing care. SaludAbierta aims to become a regional player in Spanish-speaking countries in Latin America by delivering a distinctive value proposition focused on advisory and personalization.

Historical Timeline of Events

- *2007 – The Salud Group Brand was launched to set up the largest integrated healthcare provider in Peru.*
- *2018 – The Salud Group expanded to Colombia with the setting up of the Salud Group Barranquilla and the Salud Group Medellin Sur.*
- *2021 – The Salud Group accelerated its digital presence with the setting up of Clinica Global (telehealth platform), SaludAplica (healthcare marketplace) and SaludAbierta (the e-pharmacy of the group).*
- *2021 – July: Ana Marin joined SaludAbierta to lead the initiative's launch and propose a new low-cost alternative for the underserved healthcare market in Peru.*

- *2022 – The Salud Group becomes a healthcare conglomerate with 14 branches in 7 cities in Peru and Colombia and a staff of more than 7,000 employees and qualified professionals.*

Biography of the Protagonists

Ana Marin, Venture CEO of SaludAbierta
Ana Marin joined SaludAbierta in July 2021 as Venture CEO. Before that, Ana was the Marketing Director of Glovo and then Pedidos Ya in Peru from 2019 to 2021. Before 2019, Ana Marin spent more than ten years at multinational corporations, many of which operated in the fast-moving consumer goods (FMCG) industry. She worked for names such as Alicorp, Coca-Cola and Nestle, developing her expertise in marketing and communications. Ana holds an International MBA from EADA Business School (Spain) and a Bachelor of Business Administration from Universidad del Pacífico (Peru).

Roger Lopez, Chairman of the Board
Roger Lopez has been a member of the board of directors since 2008. Mr. Lopez is Co-Founder, Chief Executive Officer, and Chairman of the board of directors of Enfoca, one of Latin America's foremost investment firms founded in 2000, where he is responsible for the investment and management of Enfoca's funds. He has more than 32 years of investment experience and, prior to founding Enfoca, he held various senior executive positions in banking and asset management, including at Banco de Crédito del Perú from 1994 to 1999, BEA Associates from 1992 to 1993 and Salomon Brothers Inc. from 1988 to 1992. Mr. Lopez holds an MBA from Columbia Business School and a Bachelor's degree in Industrial Engineering from Universidad Nacional Autónoma de México

Manuel Casanova, CEO of the Salud Group
Manuel Casanova has been a board of directors member since 2009. Before becoming the Salud Group's CEO in 2020, Mr. Casanova had served in senior roles since 2002, including as a CEO from 2009 to 2015 and as an Executive Director from 2015 to 2020. Mr. Casanova has been a member of the board of directors of Oncosalud since 2008 and that of Textil del Valle, a garment manufacturing company, since 2011. He holds a degree in Business Administration from Universidad de Lima and completed insurance courses at the MAPFRE Foundation in Spain.

Epilogue: What Really Happened at the End of this Development Journey?

The protagonist, the daughter of medical doctors, received a call in July 2021 that started to connect all the dots. Ana was approached to join private healthcare provider the Salud Group as the Venture CEO for e-pharmacy SaludAbierta. After her experience in both technology startups and established multinationals, her move to healthcare technology made her the ideal candidate to lead the recently launched (January 2021) SaludAbierta. The project aimed to be a strategic building block of the Salud Group's vision of accessible healthcare for millions of users, through a convenient set of e-pharmacy services. Ana aimed for SaludAbierta to become a regional player in Spanish-speaking countries in Latin America by delivering a distinctive value proposition focused on advisory and personalization.

The first step for the protagonist was to go through a discovery process in which an essential plain was identified. It was discovered that 90% of chronic disease patients have diabetes. Based on this, SaludAbierta's low-end project decided to focus on this disease's treatment. The second step was to define the four critical pillars by which the project will be backed up; convenience, agility, advisory and personalization. The third step was to define where to establish the experiment. Due to accessibility, it was decided to keep operations in the capital Lima. Specifically, the first trial approached five key disadvantaged districts. Two of these five districts were selected to test the project and understand the main behavioral patterns. In the end, one district (San Juan de Lurigancho) was selected to fully implement the project of treating diabetes patients through the low-end SaludAbierta formula.

The total population attended went up to 2,000 patients per week, but the actual demand was double this size, generating a significant challenge for SaludAbierta's vans delivering the treatment and service. At this stage, the only way to continue was to double the investment by the Salud Group to serve the entire segment and avoid the boycott that was starting to happen in the district. Coinciding with the third wave of the COVID-19 pandemic in Peru, the Salud Group decided to disinvest in the SaludAbierta low-end project, discontinued 60% of the total 176 that had joined the project and decided to focus the rest on other business areas of the Salud Group that attended the high end of the population.

After the divestment of the leading group on the SaludAbierta project, Ana decided to leave the company in search of a new project in which she could realize her goal of leading with a purpose while promoting positive social change.

Notes

1 Pan American Health Organization. (2021, June 24). Available at: www.paho.org/en/news/24-6-2021-183000-deaths-could-be-prevented-peru-through-prevention-and-control-noncommunicable
2 World Health Organization. (n.d.). Available at: www.who.int/news-room/fact-sheets/detail/diabetes
3 Pan American Health Organization. (2021, June 24). Available at: www.paho.org/en/news/24-6-2021-183000-deaths-could-be-prevented-peru-through-prevention-and-control-noncommunicable
4 Pan American Health Organization. (2012). Available at: www3.paho.org/hq/dmdocuments/2012/2012-hia-peru.pdf

References

Diaz, J. & Halkias, D. (2021, August 1). Reskilling and upskilling 4IR leaders in business schools through an innovative executive education ecosystem: An integrative literature review. *Social Science Research Network*. Available at SSRN: https://ssrn.com/abstract=3897059 or http://dx.doi.org/10.2139/ssrn.3897059

Supplementary Materials and Further Reading

Alvarez-Risco, A., Del-Aguila-Arcentales, S., & Yánez, J. A. (2021). Telemedicine in Peru due to the COVID-19 pandemic: Perspective from a country with limited internet access. *American Journal of Tropical Medicine and Hygiene*, *105*(1), 6–11.

Arnold, K., Mugisha, G. A., Uzoka, F. M., Imanirakiza, S., Muhumuza, C., & Bukenya, J. N. (2021, November). Development of an e-health system for improving healthcare access in developing countries. In K. Arai (Ed.), *Proceedings of the Future Technologies Conference 2021* (Vol. 2, pp. 607–616). Springer Cham.

Bizkova, T. (2021). *The 20 health tech leaders in Latin America you should know*. Latin America Reports. https://latinamericareports.com/20-health-tech-leaders-in-latin-america-you-should-know/6158/

Carrillo-Larco, R. M., Guzman-Vilca, W. C., Leon-Velarde, F., Bernabe-Ortiz, A., Jimenez, M. M., Penny, M. E., Gianella, C., Leguía, M., Tsukayama, P., Hartinger, S. M., Lescano, A. G., Cuba-Fuentes, M. S.,

Cutipe, Y., Diez-Canseco, F., Mendoza, W., Ugarte-Gil, C., Valdivia-Gago, A., Zavaleta-Cortijo, C., & Mirandabo, J. J. (n.d.). Peru – Progress in health and sciences in 200 years of independence. *The Lancet Regional Health – Americas*, *7*, Article 100148.

Diaz, A., Edgar, D., Lazaro, M., Elias, A., & Camacho, A. A. (2022). Technological solution for logistics monitoring of medicines in Peru based on IoT. In *Sciences and Humanities International Research Conference (SHIRCON)* (pp. 1–4). Institute of Electrical and Electronics Engineers (IEEE).

Fifarma. (2022). *The digital future of healthcare*. https://fifarma.org/en/the-digital-future-of-healthcare/

Fulgencio, H. (2019). E-Health for developing countries: A theoretical model grounded on literature. In S. Kadry & A. El Hami (Eds.), *E-systems for the 21st century: Concept, developments, and applications: Volume 1: E-commerce, e-decision, e-government, e-health, and social networks* (pp. 325–348). Apple Academic Press.

Gordon, D., Sherif, D., Mauricio, R., & Qasem, A. (2022). The role of social impact innovation entrepreneurship in global health. In J. Kpodonu (Ed.), *Global cardiac surgery capacity development in low and middle-income countries* (pp. 81–97). Springer Cham.

Hossain, N., Yokota, F., Sultana, N., & Ahmed, A. (2019). Factors influencing rural end-users' acceptance of e-health in developing countries: A study on portable health clinic in Bangladesh. *Telemedicine and e-Health*, *25*(3), 221–229.

Rinty, M. R., Prodhan, U. K., & Rahman, M. M. (2022). A prospective interoperable distributed e-health system with loose coupling in improving healthcare services for developing countries. *Array*, *13*, Article 100114.

Mauco, K. L., Scott, R. E., & Mars, M. (2020). Validation of an e-health readiness assessment framework for developing countries. *BMC Health Services Research*, *20*(1), Article 575.

Ruiz, E. C. V. & Sánchez, Á. J. (2019, April). E-health in Ecuador: Experiences and good practice. In *2019 Sixth International Conference on eDemocracy & eGovernment (ICEDEG)* (pp. 92–100). Institute of Electrical and Electronics Engineers (IEEE).

Trenfield, S., Awad, A., McCoubrey, L. E., Goyanes, A., Elbadawi, M., Basit, A. W., & Gaisford, S. (2022). Advancing pharmacy and healthcare with virtual digital technologies. *Advanced Drug Delivery Reviews*, *182*, Article 114098.

Stott, M. (2020). Tech offers Latin America prospect of fairer healthcare. *Financial Times*. www.ft.com/content/8ddf194c-6847-11ea-a6ac-9122541af204

Zishan, M. S. R., Mohamed, M. A., Hossain, C. A., Ahasan, R., & Sharun, S. M. (2022). Design and deployment of e-health system using machine learning in the perspective of developing countries. *International Journal of Ambient Computing and Intelligence (IJACI)*, *13*(1), 1–20.

3 United Arab Emirates: Disrupting Food Waste in the UAE

The Case of The Waste Lab

Jordi Diaz, Daphne Halkias and Tatiana Harkiolakis

"*Create an opportunity for every food scrap to become a solution*".

Setting the Stage: Unveiling The Waste Lab

Amid the United Arab Emirates' (UAE) rapid urbanization and lavish lifestyle lies a pressing challenge—an overwhelming volume of food waste. The Waste Lab, a groundbreaking startup, emerged as the brainchild of Lara Hussein, a Lebanese entrepreneur with a diverse business and hospitality management background. Lara's journey from a Bachelor's degree in Business Administration to a Master's in Hospitality Management from EADA Business School equipped her with a profound understanding of consumer behavior and market dynamics. The catalyst for her venture was the COVID-19 lockdown, which prompted her introspection on sustainability. Lara and co-founder Ceylan identified the UAE's food waste issue, which led to the inception of The Waste Lab.

Starting with a small-scale pilot in a Dubai community, The Waste Lab expanded from residential (B2C) services to business-to-business (B2B) services targeting hotels and corporations. Lara's market insight was crucial in shaping The Waste Lab's services, including waste collection, segregation training and composting. Despite early promise, The Waste Lab faced challenges, including educating the population on waste segregation, navigating regulations, securing funding and building a reliable team.

DOI: 10.4324/9781003616108-3

The Entrepreneurial Journey: Lara's Odyssey

Lara Hussein's entrepreneurial odyssey combines diverse experiences and a deep passion for sustainability. Hailing from Beirut, Lebanon, she pursued a Bachelor's in Business Administration, majoring in marketing and consumer behavior. Her academic foundation laid the groundwork for a keen understanding of market dynamics. A Master's in Hospitality Management from EADA Business School broadened her perspective on service-oriented industries.

Lara's professional versatility saw her navigate various roles in startups and multinational companies, which allowed her to acquire a unique skill set. The global onset of the COVID-19 pandemic in 2020 became a pivotal moment for Lara. Working from her Dubai home, she reflected on the pandemic's broader impacts. This introspection ignited a desire to contribute meaningfully to societal and environmental well-being and led to the inception of The Waste Lab.

Determined to address the UAE's escalating food waste problem, Lara and her co-founder left their corporate jobs to focus on developing The Waste Lab. Six months in Turkey were dedicated to testing and refining their concept, a process that was essential for adapting it to the UAE's unique environmental and market conditions. When she returned to Dubai in 2021, Lara officially commenced her startup journey.

Participating in a sustainability startup incubation program in Dubai provided essential resources, including mentorship and research capabilities. Lara faced challenges in educating the community about waste management, navigating bureaucratic hurdles and securing funding. Nevertheless, her resilience, honed through diverse professional experiences, proved vital in overcoming these obstacles.

Lara's odyssey from a business graduate to a sustainability entrepreneur is a narrative of transformation fuelled by a passion for environmental stewardship. The Waste Lab's inception is a business story and a testament to entrepreneurial vision driving meaningful change. Lara's journey serves as an inspiration for aspiring entrepreneurs seeking to make a difference in sustainability.

Brief Literature Review on Global Food Waste Challenges

Food waste in developed countries is a significant issue with far-reaching implications (Kim et al., 2019). The prevalence of food waste in developed countries is relatively high, representing a significant proportion of global food waste. In developed countries, much of the food produced is never consumed. Estimates suggest that around 30% to 40% of all food produced is wasted in regions like North America and Europe (Vogiatzi, 2023). This food waste includes food lost in the supply chain and food thrown away by consumers (Amicarelli et al., 2022).

Most food waste in developed countries occurs at the consumer level, unlike in developing countries, where food waste is more likely to happen at the production or storage stages (Valero i Solé, 2022). In households, food is often wasted due to over-purchasing, poor planning, confusion over expiration dates and a lack of awareness about storing and using leftovers (Begho & Zhao, 2023). In developed countries, consumers often buy more food than they need. Factors such as large portion sizes, the availability of inexpensive food and a culture of abundance contribute to this behavior. Furthermore, strict aesthetic standards for fruits and vegetables lead to the rejection of perfectly edible items that are not visually appealing (Amaral & Orsato, 2023; Pagliarini et al., 2024).

Many consumers in developed countries are not fully aware of the impact of food waste, including a lack of understanding about storing food properly, using leftovers and the difference between "best before" and "use by" dates on packaging (Schrank et al., 2023). The relative affordability of food in developed countries can lead to a devaluation of its worth. People may not perceive waste as a significant loss when food is cheap (Begho & Zhao, 2023). Supermarkets, restaurants and hotels in developed countries also contribute substantially to food waste due to overstocking, cosmetic standards for produce, buffet-style servings, and large portion sizes (Juvan et al., 2023; Lagioia et al., 2024).

Food waste can occur anywhere in the supply chain, from farm to table. Inefficiencies in harvesting, processing, transporting and storing food can result in significant waste (Valero i Solé, 2022). Inadequate policies and infrastructure can exacerbate food waste, such as a lack of composting facilities, inadequate food donation systems and policies that create barriers to food redistribution (Vogiatzi, 2023). The economic cost of this waste is significant and affects the cost of resources used in production, such as water, land, energy, labor and capital investment (Kim et al., 2019). Food waste contributes to greenhouse gas emissions in terms of the methane released by food decomposing in landfills, the carbon footprint of producing food that is never eaten and the waste of resources like water and arable land (Juvan et al., 2023).

While developed countries are wasting a substantial amount of food, there are still issues with food insecurity and poverty within these countries (Schrank et al., 2023). This paradox highlights the need for better food distribution and donation systems (Amicarelli et al., 2022). Some developed countries have started addressing the issue through policies and initiatives to reduce food waste, encourage food donation, improve consumer awareness and encourage behavior modification and changes in industry practices (Kim et al., 2019).

Food waste in the UAE is a significant concern, reflecting a broader issue prevalent in many affluent nations (Osaili et al., 2022). Several factors contribute to this issue in the UAE. The UAE has a high per capita income and a consumer culture that favors abundance and luxury, leading to excessive food purchases and, consequently, higher levels of waste (El Bilali & Ben Hassen, 2020). The hospitality sector in the UAE, which includes numerous high-end hotels and restaurants, often contributes to food waste through large buffet spreads and portion sizes (Kennedy et al., 2023). Similarly, retail outlets may discard food items that do not meet aesthetic standards (El Bilali & Ben Hassen, 2020).

Cultural practices, especially during festivals and celebrations like Ramadan and weddings, often involve preparing large quantities of food. A significant portion of this food can end up as food waste (Osaili et al., 2022). Consumers in the UAE often lack awareness about the environmental and economic impacts of food waste and lack understanding about proper food storage and management (Kennedy et al., 2023). The UAE imports a large percentage of its food, raising concerns about the sustainability of its food system. The long supply chains in food importation can increase food spoilage and waste (El Bilali & Ben Hassen, 2020).

The UAE government has recognized this issue and has started implementing strategies to combat food waste (Kennedy et al., 2023). These strategies include public awareness campaigns, waste reduction initiatives in the hospitality sector and collaborations with food banks for food redistribution (Kennedy et al., 2023). The UAE is also exploring technological and innovative solutions to tackle food waste, such as smart apps to track and reduce waste and initiatives to recycle food waste into renewable energy or compost (Osaili et al., 2022).

The environmental impact of food waste in the UAE is significant, particularly considering the country's arid climate and limited water resources (El Bilali & Ben Hassen, 2020). Reducing food waste is critical in promoting sustainability and reducing the ecological footprint. Additionally, a movement is growing around more sustainable practices, like composting and using "ugly" fruits and vegetables (Osaili et al., 2022). Food waste in the UAE is a multifaceted issue influenced by cultural, economic and social factors. Addressing it requires policy intervention, technological innovation and changes in consumer behavior and business practices (Kennedy et al., 2023).

The UAE's efforts in reducing food waste are ongoing and evolving (Kennedy et al., 2023). The consequences of food waste are not limited to the direct loss of food. It also has environmental impacts, such as the unnecessary use of water, land and energy resources, and contributes to greenhouse gas emissions when wasted food decomposes in landfills (Schrank et al., 2023). Addressing food waste in developed countries requires a multifaceted approach, including consumer education, improved food storage and distribution systems, changes in food labeling practices and policies promoting food donation and waste reduction (Kim et al., 2019).

The Protagonists' Dilemma: Unraveling the Sustainability Challenges and Food Waste in the UAE

Upon returning to the UAE and founding The Waste Lab, Lara and Ceylan were confronted with alarming facts about the country's waste issues. Food waste in the UAE proved to be more complex and pervasive than imagined, with numerous factors making the UAE one of the top global contributors to food waste per capita. The UAE generates a staggering 3.27 million tons of food waste annually, equivalent to over 6.5 times the weight of the Burj Khalifa, the world's tallest building. This staggering figure illustrates the issue's magnitude, with food wastage comprising approximately 38% of daily prepared food and 40% of the average household waste. Regarding per capita waste generation, the UAE significantly surpasses Europe, producing an average of 2.7 kg compared to Europe's 1.2 kg.

The financial toll of food waste in the UAE is substantial, costing a whopping USD 3.5 billion. This figure surpasses half the annual cost of food imports, USD 6.4 billion, representing nearly 1.0% of the country's GDP. The disposed food waste ends up in landfills, releasing harmful gases like methane, a potent contributor to climate change. In response to landfill issues, the UAE government took decisive action by drastically increasing the waste disposal cost and implementing different fees for recyclable and non-recyclable waste. While this aligns with the government's commendable goal to reduce landfill waste by 80–90%, it has a noticeable impact on the cost of living. Consequently, there is a pressing need for a comprehensive solution to manage food waste at its source.

Complementing this challenge is the rise in compost prices, affecting farmers and consumers alike. Since 90% of the UAE's compost relies on imports, increased prices strain farmers' profit margins and impact consumers' budgets, potentially contributing to overall inflation in the food sector. This phenomenon underscores the critical need for local compost facilities to reduce import dependence. Crucially, the UAE's commitment to global sustainability objectives, exemplified in forums like COP 28, which took place in Dubai in December 2023, emphasizes the urgency of effective food waste solutions. Beyond environmental concerns, food waste in the UAE poses substantial economic and social challenges, underscoring the need for immediate action involving governmental initiatives, sustainability-driven businesses and public engagement. These efforts are essential to foster responsible and sustainable food disposal practices and to address the multifaceted challenges posed by food waste in the UAE. Lara and Ceylan's journey to address the intricate issue of food waste in the UAE reflects a dedication to environmental sustainability and an acute awareness of the economic and social ramifications. As the UAE grapples with the pervasive issue of food waste, the facts presented illuminate the urgency of finding solutions and the collective responsibility needed to navigate these challenges.

The Waste Lab Unveiled: From Pilot to Disruptive Solutions

> "The Waste Lab is a home-grown, women-owned, and impact-driven startup that is working with households and businesses to create an opportunity for every food scrap to become a solution for rather than a burden on our society and environment—through nature-based composting and repurposing solutions".
>
> (The Waste Lab, 2024)

Lara and Ceylan's journey began in 2021 after founding The Waste Lab in Dubai. However, how do you find the first customers? What do the processes look like in reality? An incubation program in Dubai that provided support for startups with a sustainability focus held the answers. This program included mentorship, research and idea testing for startups, and it became the perfect opportunity to develop the idea further and test the product on real customers. The first customers were mainly expatriates—people from other countries living and working in Dubai—who were already used to separating waste in their home countries. In cooperation with the incubation program, Lara and Ceylan were able to start collecting food waste from around 500 households, each household consisting of 4–5 people. The direct exchange with the people helped to adapt and further develop the product and the processes constantly.

The positive feedback resulted in the first paid B2C subscriptions, where the bins were collected once a week or by appointment with customers. The services offered included training sessions (what belongs in the bin?) and impact reports (reduction of CO2 emissions, compost production in kg). These face-to-face communications shaped customer loyalty, empowered people to celebrate small steps and helped them understand their direct impact. The process works as follows: the segregated bins are collected and taken to the control station. Unlike other waste management companies that recycle food waste without separating it, The Waste Lab separates diverse kinds of food before recycling it. The compostable waste is further processed in the compost station, resulting in end products such as compost and biochar. Partners who use food waste for animal feed production or other purposes, such as growing mushrooms, reuse the non-compostable part of the waste. At every stage of the process, The Waste Lab tracks data from food waste collection to retreatment and gives impact reporting based on that data. "We have talked to so many people, residents, and businesses, and one of the things lacking is transparency and local data", Lara said (personal communication, February 4, 2024).

Initially, the land for compost production was provided as part of the deal with the incubator program. However, it quickly became a challenge as more extensive land areas would be needed as the company grew its operations. It took Lara and Ceylan two years to find suitable land. The problem of limited space for compost was solved by a local Emirati landowner who made part of his farm available for their activities, allowing the daily processing of 17 tons of food waste. Only around 20% of the 5000m^2 land area capacity is being used. The Waste Lab's limited financial resources could be preserved as the land was only rented and not purchased. The company entered the B2B space in 2022 to reduce ecological vulnerability and increase community awareness about carbon footprints on a larger scale. These activities grew organically; as in the beginning, engaged private customers requested their companies to collaborate with The Waste Lab. All B2C and B2B activities led to 500 paid subscriptions in the first year.

At the end of 2022, Lara and Ceylan started pilot projects with four Hilton Hotels to further test and develop their processes in the B2B business, with a focus on HORECA (hospitality, restaurant and catering) channels. As those hotels had no data about their food waste, one month of data assessment was necessary to evaluate the amount of food waste generated, followed by a proposal for the forecasted number of bins, pickup schedule and costs. The onboarding program's next step was training the kitchen workforce to reduce the number of incorrectly separated food scraps that cannot be composted. Giving the workforce feedback could lower waste contamination from 15% to 5%. Every hotel received a report with data analysis to measure their impact. B2B leftovers and food scraps can range from 500 kg to 3,000 kg per month, in contrast to B2C food wastes that range from 20 kg to 25 kg per month.

After the successful pilot projects, one major challenge is raising seed investments to scale up the operations, automate processes, expand the team and grow as more demand comes from B2B customers such as hotels. The Waste Lab's goal is a 10% increase in composted waste every month, resulting in more than 3 million kg of food waste composted every month by the end of the year 2026 (which accounts for only 1% of the total food waste of the UAE). Another main challenge for the company will be whether compost sales can be another essential revenue stream. The first successful trials with local farmers were conducted while compost prices increased over the last few years (around 90% of compost in the UAE is imported).

The company's goal is not only to focus on food waste in the United Arab Emirates but also to generate awareness throughout the region through partnerships and consulting services. One milestone to build upon is the partnership with the global automotive company Kia in April 2023. The Waste Lab and Kia have partnered to raise awareness and mobilize individuals around the global issue of food waste while guiding them towards practical solutions. The partnership started at the beginning of Ramadan, nudging consumers to rethink their practices and mindset around food wastage.

Of the partnership, Yaser Shabsogh, Chief Operating Officer of the Middle East & Africa Regional HQ of Kia, said, "We aim to shift people's mindset around food waste and responsible consumption. We understand that this commitment can transform our world and bring the cycle of life full circle" (Quraishi, 2023, para. 6).

Lara and Ceylan also stated, "By emphasizing the advantages of sourcing locally and minimizing food waste, we can raise awareness and promote responsible consumption. We are grateful to Kia for supporting and collaborating on this impactful movement" (Quraishi, 2023, para. 9).

Navigating Dilemmas: Securing Investor Confidence

Fresh off the success and excitement of the COP 28 partnership, Lara Hussein, the co-founder of The Waste Lab, faced a stark reality on her journey home. Despite the company reaching the break-even point, financial constraints loomed large, threatening to impede The Waste Lab's potential for growth. Celebrating successful partnerships is juxtaposed with the persistent challenge of securing funding to scale operations, automate processes and address the increasing demand in the B2B sector. Lara reflected on the current state of The Waste Lab, thinking about how she grapples with multiple business lines—B2C, B2B and marketing campaigns like the one with Kia. Although the company was breaking even, talent retention had become a pressing concern due to the company's inability to offer competitive salaries. The high turnover posed a challenge, diverting Lara's attention from strategic endeavors.

Moreover, with a diverse portfolio of business models, Lara encountered difficulty in presenting a clear narrative to investors. One important investor had provided feedback expressing a lack of clarity regarding the problem The Waste Lab aims to solve, for whom and why The Waste Lab was the best solution. The ambiguity in articulating the value proposition became a crucial challenge to which Lara had yet to respond. She struggled to effectively demonstrate to potential investors that The Waste Lab was a disruptive innovation in the UAE, actively addressing a significant market need. Furthermore, how could she showcase that the business was positioned for substantial growth and held the potential for lucrative returns in the future?

As Lara Hussein steadfastly believed in the transformative potential of The Waste Lab and witnessed a rising tide of awareness surrounding the critical issue of food waste, she found herself navigating a landscape laden with myriad responsibilities. The overwhelming array of tasks she faced included day-to-day operations and strategic decisions and the demanding endeavor of substantiating The Waste Lab's intrinsic value to potential investors. In this intricate balancing act, Lara strived to secure the necessary support to foster growth while endeavoring to sustain the flame of her entrepreneurial dream.

Epilogue

Lara and Ceylan's startup was met with success during its early stages. Nevertheless, presenting a clear pitch to investors and securing funding to scale operations, automate processes, address increasing demand in the B2B sector and offer competitive salaries remained challenging. Lara was determined to continue to seek funding and ensure The Waste Lab's growth. She started entering pitch competitions, applying for venture capital funding and looking into entrepreneurial development programs. Each experience pushed her to define her narrative and value proposition better.

Her efforts paid off when The Waste Lab began gaining international recognition. By 2023, The Waste Lab had saved half a million tons of food waste from landfills. In February 2024, Lara was nominated by the Boston Consulting Group for the V60 Awards, which celebrate Visionary Women in Climate & Sustainability in the Middle East. Later that same month, The Waste Lab won third place, tied with another startup, in the UAE cohort of a pitch competition hosted by the Atlantic Council and Georgetown University McDonough School of Business. The win led to securing a place in the WIn Fellowship, a sponsored year-long development program for women entrepreneurs in the MENA region. Around the same time, The Waste Lab was selected as one of several semi-finalists for the Regenerative Agriculture Venture Programme by Goumbook in partnership with HSBC and HSBC Saudi Arabia and funded partly by the European Union.

The startup's original B2B pilot projects with Hilton Hotels led to a flourishing partnership with five Hilton Hotels in Dubai. The startup's impact reports demonstrated that the hotels saved over 80,000 kilos of food scraps and leftovers from landfills and prevented over 90,000 kilos of CO_2 emissions in one month alone. That amount of CO_2 emissions is equivalent to consuming over 40,000 liters of gasoline or charging 11 million smartphones.

Lara's determination to stick to her entrepreneurial vision and her proactive approach to seeking funding, development and exposure paid off. The unique value of her business lies not only in its sustainable and innovative approach to food waste management but also in its strategy of taking a community-focused approach that involves citizens, businesses, schools and other institutions in regenerating local ecosystems. The Waste Lab's partnerships extended beyond businesses like Kia to include international sustainability alliances such as The Alliance for Sustainable Schools. Her dream continues to grow and make a positive impact on sustainability in the UAE, with her efforts being recognized and lauded globally.

Acknowledgements

The authors wish to acknowledge Ms. Lara Hussein's contribution in providing information for this case study and also acknowledge EADA Business School students Lean Hui Juan, Ramos Da Silva Diego, Richards Diego Ignacio, Salinas Ana Paula, Singh Digvijay and Tremel Julian, who developed the preparatory information for this case study as part of their course requirements.

References

Amaral, D. G. & Orsato, R. J. (2023). Digital platforms for food waste reduction: The value for business users. *Business Strategy and the Environment*, *32*(4), 1373–1387. https://doi.org/10.1002/bse.3193

Amicarelli, V., Aluculesei, A. C., Lagioia, G., Pamfilie, R., & Bux, C. (2022). How to manage and minimize food waste in the hotel industry: An exploratory research. *International Journal of Culture, Tourism and Hospitality Research*, *16*(1), 152–167. https://doi.org/10.1108/IJCTHR-01-2021-0019

Begho, T. & Zhao, N. (2023). Motivating household food waste reduction: Harnessing the power of message context and framing. *Food Frontiers*, *4*(1), 432–446. https://doi.org/10.1002/fft2.193

El Bilali, H. & Ben Hassen, T. (2020). Food waste in the countries of the Gulf Cooperation Council: A systematic review. *Foods*, *9*(4), Article 463. https://doi.org/10.3390/foods9040463

Juvan, E., Grün, B., & Dolnicar, S. (2023). Waste production patterns in hotels and restaurants: An intra-sectoral segmentation approach. *Annals of Tourism Research Empirical Insights*, *4*(1), Article 100090. https://doi.org/10.1016/j.annale.2023.100090

Kennedy, L., Safi, S., Osaili, T. M., Al Rajabi, A., Alblooshi, A., Al Jawarneh, D., Al Kaabi, A., Al Rubael, F., Albreiki, M., Alfadli, M., Alhefeiti, A., Faris, M. A. I. E., Allaham, K., Junaidi, S., & Khan, M. A. B. (2023). The attitudes and practices of United Arab Emirates consumers towards food waste: A nationwide cross-sectional study [version 2; peer review: 2 approved]. *F1000Research, 12*, Article 911. https://doi.org/10.12688/f1000research.135678.2

Kim, J., Rundle-Thiele, S., & Knox, K. (2019). Systematic literature review of best practice in food waste reduction programs. *Journal of Social Marketing, 9*(4), 447–466. https://doi.org/10.1108/JSOCM-05-2019-0074

Lagioia, G., Amicarelli, V., Strippoli, R., Bux, C., & Gallucci, T. (2024). Sustainable and circular practices in the hotel industry in Southern Italy: Opportunities, barriers and trends in food waste management. *British Food Journal, 126*(1), 428–452. https://doi.org/10.1108/BFJ-12-2022-1144

Osaili, T. M., Obaid, R. S., Alqutub, R., Akkila, R., Habil, A., Dawoud, A., Duhair, S., Hasan, F., Hashim, M., Cheikh Ismail, L., Al-Nabulsi, A. A., & Taha, S. (2022). Food wastage attitudes among the United Arab Emirates population: The role of social media. *Sustainability, 14*(3), Article 1870. https://doi.org/10.3390/su14031870

Pagliarini, E., Minichiello, C., Sisti, L., Totaro, G., Baffoni, L., Di Gioia, D., & Saccani, A. (2024). From food waste to eco-friendly functionalized polymer composites: Investigation of orange peels as active filler. *New Biotechnology, 80*, 37–45. https://doi.org/10.1016/j.nbt.2024.01.001

Quraishi, N. (2023, April 27). *Kia partners with The Waste Lab to launch 'Cycle of Life' campaign tackling food waste.* Campaign Middle East. https://campaignme.com/kia-partners-with-the-waste-lab-to-launch-cycle-of-life-campaign-tackling-food-waste/

Schrank, J., Hanchai, A., Thongsalab, S., Sawaddee, N., Chanrattanagorn, K., & Ketkaew, C. (2023). Factors of food waste reduction underlying the extended theory of planned behavior: A study of consumer behavior towards the intention to reduce food waste. *Resources, 12*(8), Article 93. https://doi.org/10.3390/resources12080093

The Waste Lab. (2024). *The Waste Lab pitch deck* (confidential).

Valero i Solé, O. (2022). *Artificial intelligence and blockchain for food loss and waste prevention and reduction* [Bachelor's thesis, Pompeu Fabra University]. UPF Digital Repository. http://hdl.handle.net/10230/54898

Vogiatzi, V. (2023). *Meleti tou fenomenou tis spatalis trofimon stin efodiastiki tous alisida ke diereunisi ton praktikon antimetopisis tis me ti hrisi tou Diadiktiou ton Pragmaton (IoT) ke tis tehnologias blockchain* [A study on the phenomenon of food waste in their supply chain and investigating methods of dealing with it using Internet of Things (IoT) and blockchain technology] [Bachelor's thesis, National Technical University of Athens]. DSpace@NTUA. http://dx.doi.org/10.26240/heal.ntua.25494

Supplemental Reading

Alomar, D. (2022, August 27). The Waste Lab onboards corporate titans to fight food waste. *Arab News*. www.arabnews.com/node/2151531/business-economy

Chandran, S. (2022, March 2). How the UAE is solving the problem of food waste. *Gulf News*. https://gulfnews.com/friday/art- people/how-uae-is-solving-the-problem-of-food-waste-1.2314565

Staff Writer. (2018, February 8). *Dubai announces new waste disposal fees*. Gulf Business. https://gulfbusiness.com/dubai-announces-new-waste-disposal-fees

4 Spain: Challenging Established Norms

Wine in a Can, Inc. and Disruptive Innovation in the Wine Industry

Jordi Diaz, Daphne Halkias and Tatiana Harkiolakis

Following an intense three-year span, Nour Aziz reached a pivotal juncture, recognizing the imperative to formulate a sustainable strategy. As a hardworking entrepreneur engaged in round-the-clock operations—managing sales, packaging, negotiations with distributors and producers and a continuous pursuit of funding to address cash flow exigencies—she began to acknowledge the tangible constraints her body was signaling. While unwavering in her belief in the "Wine in a Can idea", she concurrently grasped the necessity for a more enduring and sustainable strategic framework.

Biography and Developmental Background of the Protagonist

Nour Aziz is the eldest daughter of three siblings, born to Moroccan immigrants. She had a difficult childhood, raised in a conservative religious family; she started working when she was 13. As a teenager, she was diagnosed with an autoimmune disease. After being treated for some time, she left for India, looking for a cure. While in India, she reached a turning point in her life and found a career pathway after being in between jobs for years.

Returning from India, she enrolled in EADA's MBA program, where she discovered her interest in Islamic Finance, and took a summer course in the UK. Nour started a job with an Islamic Finance consulting company in 2012 but soon realized that consulting was not for her. Leaving the consulting industry, she joined a project with EADA Business School to develop software focused on learning skills for children with autism, which gave her a new perspective on business.

DOI: 10.4324/9781003616108-4

In 2013, the Chamber of Commerce in Barcelona invited her to be a moderator for a summit on Islamic Finance, giving her background in the Middle Eastern business industry. During the summit, she was recruited by a US investment fund for a wine bodega in Priorat despite having no previous knowledge of the wine industry. This position made her discover an industry that became part of her life. At 24 years old, Nour acquired enough skills at the wine bodega to play a critical role in establishing its operations and was promoted to COO. She created a new employee team, company culture, branding and structure. Having worked for four years on the software project, Nour realized there was little room for her to grow. She could not be promoted to CEO since she was not a vintner. Additionally, her family was not pleased with her job, as alcoholic drinks were against her family's religious beliefs.

Nour's love for the world of wine began in 2013 when she embarked on the relaunch of a winery based in the Priorat wine region. Their love for wine made her even produce wine at home for friends. With her innovative personality and determination to grow, Nour received a scholarship at IESE Business School in NYC and left the winery. In 2019, her friends introduced Nour Aziz to canned wine in New York. She looked for the wine in her friend's fridge but could not find the bottle. Nour had never considered wine in a different packaging, such as a can, and was surprised to find canned wine, but it tasted good once she tried it.

After this experience, the wine in a can captivated her. Nour started to investigate. She talked to winemakers, winegrowers and consumers and began looking for information about canning, its characteristics and the opportunities this new packaging could provide for wine. What followed was the birth of Wine in a Can in March 2020. Founded by the young entrepreneur Nour Aziz, Wine in a Can aimed to revolutionize the wine industry by offering canned and organic wine. Under the slogan 'a sip of freedom', Wine in a Can's goal is not to challenge bottled wine but to push the wine industry into new ways and occasions of consumption that the bottle cannot reach. Under the principle of freedom, Nour also selects her investors. They should support her in networking and marketing her brand and, more importantly, understand her story.

Nour offers four Wine in a Can vegan and organic Grenache wines: vino blanco, vino tinto, vino rosado and sparkling wine. Transparent in its ingredients and production process, Wine in a Can prioritizes the quality of its products and makes a conscious selection of the grapes. She intended to single-can varieties of the best Spanish varieties, showing the new consumer the extraordinary national raw material. Disruptive and environmentally conscious, Wine in a Can does not stick to specific targets but is based on attitudes while responding to new trends in the sector. Wine in a Can significantly grows young and organic wines in pick-and-go formats. The target group of Wine in a Can consumers is a mix of citizens worldwide: urban consumers, digital shoppers, consumers of food deliveries, consumers of social media, especially Instagram, and people who care about their health but without excesses. Wine in a Can talks about attitudes and goes beyond age, race and gender.

Rebellious, young, honest and dreamy describe Wine in a Can best. Wine in a Can provides a positive change that encourages consumers to overcome any complexes to enjoy wine wherever and whenever they want. As a responsible and environmentally sustainable company, Wine in a Can uses aluminum cans that are 100% recyclable, which results in a small environmental footprint compared to that of glass bottles. The labels are made of paper to give the consumer a luxurious feeling and make it easy to write their name.

Background Information on the Product: The Wine-in-a-Can Market

Recent studies indicate a shift in consumer perceptions, particularly among Gen Z and Millennial generations, leading to winemakers experimenting with alternative packaging to stand out in the competitive retail landscape. The contemporary wine consumer exhibits a growing preference for convenient, vibrant, functional and eco-friendly alternative wine packaging, as highlighted in Montalvo-Falcón et al.'s (2023) research. Such alternative packaging deviates from the traditional 750ml glass bottle, encompassing a variety of containers such as Tetra Packs, wine-on-tap, bag-in-box, mini aluminum cans and individual serving-sized plastic pouches.

Winemakers, both large- and small-scale, are exploring these alternative packaging options to cater to expanding wine consumption occasions and locations while differentiating their products on crowded retail shelves. These alternative packaging methods address consumer and distributor concerns regarding convenience, portion control and quality. Notably, the wine-in-a-can option offers the unique advantage of 360-degree individualized branding messages, resonating strongly with today's Instagram-focused wine consumers (Ruggeri et al., 2022).

Controversial design innovation influences the adoption of alternative packaging (Ben-Slimane, K., & Fessi, 2023). The concept is not entirely new in the context of wine-in-a-can, given the longstanding use of cans for beverages like soda, juice and beer. However, given wine's complexity and the challenge of assessing its quality before consumption, the can represents a less radical yet innovative packaging choice. Wine's cachet often relies on branded images and the overall product and corporate brand identity (Dua et al., 2023).

Wine consumers typically depend on extrinsic cues like wine labels, descriptions and branded reputation. The 360-degree design of wine-in-a-can allows winemakers to offer both intrinsic (image identification) and extrinsic (informational) cues, assisting consumers in mitigating social and financial risks associated with wine selection and purchase. Previous research suggests that the more consumers are involved in using and purchasing a product like wine, the less they depend on extrinsic cues for perception formation and acceptance of the product category (Csiba-Herczeg et al., 2023). Thus, the degree of radicalness, the information provided and the consumers' involvement with the product category innovation (such as wine-in-a-can) influence the acceptance of such innovation. In a highly competitive and saturated market, winemakers aiming to introduce innovative, more convenient packaging solutions like wine-in-a-can can positively influence the global wine market's overall growth trajectory (Versari et al., 2023).

Wine in a Can: Company History and Profile

Wine in a Can considers beer as their direct competitor instead of bottled wine. The company is not trying to change the behavior of the wine-bottle consumers; instead, they are focusing on taking wine to places a wine glass cannot be taken to.

The annual household expenditure on beer increased by 35% from 2019 to 2020. Per capita expenditure on beer jumped from almost €24 in 2019 to more than €32 in 2020. Per capita expenditure on wine jumped from almost €23 in 2019 to more than €28 in 2020.

From 2016 to 2019, the alcoholic beverage market has shown steady growth (CAGR +2.1%). However, in 2020, the pandemic caused a 15% drop in consumption. Moreover, in 2021, the market showed an important recuperation but was still below pre-pandemic levels. Nevertheless, the market forecast anticipates a steady recovery and reaching pre-pandemic levels by 2023. This forecast represents a massive opportunity for the newborn Wine in a Can to snowball quickly in Spain and the international market. Nour's idea was to sell wine in cans, but not of lesser quality than wine in bottles. On the contrary, she wants high-quality wines in cans.

In the world of wine, consumers tend to associate the size, type of packaging and color with the quality of the wine, so she knew that some consumers would be prejudiced against canned wine; this represented one of the first challenges for the young company. The upcoming decisions were going to be very important for the brand.

One of the first decisions was not to produce the wine alone but to hire industrial partners. Considering this, Nour realized that to make their product known and position it as an excellent-quality wine, they needed the consumer to get to know the product first by feeling the packaging and tasting the wine. It was not enough to see it on a shelf for sale in a supermarket, and selling a product in supermarkets has very high costs for the manufacturers, which made Nour decide that supermarkets would not be their first distribution channel. Instead, she decided to go another route and sell her canned wine online by selling through Glovo, Amazon and her website.

She added Spanish airports, train stations and gas stations as her next sales channel to reach a greater audience and offer easy access to her products. The business plan did not include international projection as an early step when starting the company. Nonetheless, when Wine in a Can started distributing at travel hubs, Nour received numerous requests from people from different countries to sell the brand in their respective countries through her website, Instagram and LinkedIn page.

Despite Wine in a Can's investors initially being reluctant to launch in additional countries, Nour saw an opportunity for their company and seized it immediately. After only two years in the business, Wine in a Can became an international brand, gaining more awareness globally, and visitors from 111 countries are viewing their website. The company became present in several countries worldwide, such as Spain, the Netherlands, France, Finland, the UK, Germany, Italy, the US, Mexico, Colombia, Morocco and other African countries, launching a new market in Japan as well.

The Protagonist's Dilemma

Wine in a Can is a wine industry disrupter, facing several major dilemmas. Firstly, the most significant dilemma for the company is getting its product onto the market. Making people aware of the new way of enjoying wine, in a can, is difficult for a young company with few resources. Understanding their slice of the market and being self-aware of the resources needed to disrupt a traditional industry such as bottled wine can be a far reach in demanding times with inflation, increasing prices and energy crises.

Wine in a Can is competing not only with the wine bottle market but, more importantly, with beer cans. During 2016–2021, beer sales in Spain were more than three times higher than wine sales. While having the opportunity to take part in the market share of beer consumers, Wine in a Can needs to educate the beer market to choose wine cans as an alternative. The company does not produce its wine. Not being vertically integrated always brings challenges via relying too much on one's suppliers.

By depending on suppliers' prices, Wine in a Can needs to increase its prices despite its central vision of offering affordable, high-quality canned wine. Finally, Nour had to lay off her entire sales team because they were inefficient. The team was not working as she expected and was not getting the results Wine in a Can needed. Now Nour is alone in the Sales Division and endures a lot of pressure and stress. She gets sick regularly and is trying to figure out how to hire people she can trust and get the results she expects. This problem is seriously affecting her personal life. In the last four months, she has become ill due to stress in ways she could never have imagined. One time, it was so bad that half of her face was paralyzed for three days. She needs rest and someone to help her manage the company.

Is There a Business Opportunity for Wine in a Can to Capture Market Share?

A short-term goal for Nour is to build a strong sales team, allowing the company to expand through distribution channels. Furthermore, Wine in a Can focuses the following year on not being profitable rather than gaining market share, acquiring awareness for its product and selling to a growing audience. To pursue that, they plan to raise 1 million euros in 2023.

Within the next three years, Wine in a Can plans to invest 3 million euros in reducing costs and building its production line. Regarding costs, the company's question is: what is the minimum cost of the cans that allows the company to sell their wine at the minimum price to retailers/end-consumers while facing increasing prices due to inflation and the energy crisis? Wine in a Can being a disruptive startup, Nour must be constantly aware of potential risks or issues. The key to the future is to scale with intention and remain conscious of current and future market conditions.

References and Supplementary Materials

Ben-Slimane, K., Diridollou, C., & Hamadache, K. (2020). The legitimation strategies of early-stage disruptive innovation. *Technological Forecasting and Social Change*, *158*, Article 120161.

Ben-Slimane, K. & Fessi, L. (2023). Market shaping through controversial innovation. *International Journal of Market Research*, *65*(5), 524–531.

Bousquet, J. (2023). Marketing challenges and trends influencing wine producers and consumers. *Journal of Business and Management Studies*, *5*(3), 155–160.

Christensen, C. M., Hall, T., Dillon, K., & Duncan, D. S. (2016). Know your customers' 'jobs to be done'. *Harvard Business Review*, *94*(9), 54–62.

Christensen, C. M., Raynor, M., & McDonald, R. (2015). What is disruptive innovation? *Harvard Business Review*. https://hbr.org/2015/12/what-is-disruptive-innovation

Christensen, C. M. (1997). *The innovator's dilemma: When new technologies cause great firms to fail*. Harvard Business School Press.

Csiba-Herczeg, A., Csiba, P., Koteczki, R., & Balassa, B. E. (2023). Consumer acceptance and rejection regarding sustainable wine packaging. *Chemical Engineering Transactions*, *107*, 559–564.

Dua, S., Sahai, C., & Anekar, K. (2023). To study the evolution of wine: Bottle to can. *ATITHYA: A Journal of Hospitality*, *9*(1), 1–19.

King, A. A. & Baatartogtokh, B. (2015). How useful is the theory of disruptive innovation? *MIT Sloan Management Review*, *57*(1), 77–90.

Markides, C. (2006). Disruptive innovation: In need of better theory. *Journal of Product Innovation Management*, *23*(1), 19–25.

Montalvo-Falcón, J. V., Sánchez-García, E., Marco-Lajara, B., & Martínez-Falcó, J. (2023). Sustainability research in the wine industry: A bibliometric approach. *Agronomy*, *13*(3), 871.

Ruggeri, G., Mazzocchi, C., Corsi, S., & Ranzenigo, B. (2022). No more glass bottles? Canned wine and Italian consumers. *Foods*, *11*(8), Article 1106.

Scollary, G. R. (2021). Grapevine: Wine in a can, perhaps? *Chemistry in Australia*, *40*, 1–40.

Squire, S. (2020). Bottling and canning: Making wine for cans: What you need to know. *Australian and New Zealand Grapegrower and Winemaker*, (673), 59–60.

Versari, A., Ricci, A., Moreno, C. P., & Parpinello, G. P. (2023). Packaging of wine in aluminum cans–A review. *American Journal of Enology and Viticulture*, *74*(2), 1–12.

5 India: AI in Diagnostics and Healthcare Accessibility

The Disruptive Model of Larkai Healthcare

Jordi Diaz, Daphne Halkias and Tatiana Harkiolakis

Being explorative and adventurous from his young days, being inspired by his surroundings and naturally inclined towards healthcare and being motivated by an able mentor, guide and support, Pritam, aged 28 years, took the leap of faith and entered the world of entrepreneurship. Believing in "The how is easy if the why is powerful", he had a clear idea of what his end goal was, besides being absolutely determined, motivated and optimally confident in his abilities to give shape and life to his idea. Buckling up for the undulating terrain ahead, with a rigorous market survey of the gaps in healthcare and realizing the potential of the ever-expanding scope in cardiac care, he focused his product on being diagnostic and preventive rather than a cure and focused on making healthcare affordable, accessible and non-invasive, without compromising on the factors of comprehensive detection and diagnosis. What inspired him exponentially in taking this giant leap was the logarithmic potential of artificial intelligence in healthcare, and thereby, he began his journey of sowing, nurturing and giving birth to Larkai.

Background Information on Digital Health Technologies and Entrepreneurship in Developing Economies

An increase in the volume and variety of medical services available, tightening national and international legislation in the industry and growing demand from consumers are driving forward notable changes in the healthcare industry (Kulkova et al., 2023). An increase in the number of patients causes medical personnel to endure a growing and unpredictable workload despite the need to provide high-quality

DOI: 10.4324/9781003616108-5

services to individual patients (Mathur & Sutton, 2017). While nations are continually increasing funding for national health systems and competition is growing in the healthcare industry, companies producing medical solutions and products attempt to bring novelties to the market at a fast speed (Tarkkala et al., 2019).

The healthcare industry can respond to these pressing challenges now and in the future if it embraces technological change (Tortorella et al., 2022). Technology entrepreneurs can respond with greater speed to new challenges with increased scalability and flexibility in delivering services through their in-depth understanding of the healthcare industry, the technological tools they are using and the policy environment in which they will operate (Lee & Yoon, 2021). Understanding national and international healthcare industry regulations is especially crucial for digital healthcare startups, as regulations can enable or constrain the degree and type of innovation possible in healthcare technology (Cozzolino & Geiger, 2024).

Developing economies present unique opportunities and challenges in the nexus of entrepreneurship and digital health technologies. Better access to healthcare products and services, increased quality of care and lower costs can be enabled by the diffusion of digital health technologies in developing economies (Preko et al., 2020). Nevertheless, enabling policy environments and entrepreneurial initiatives have a notable effect on how effectively these technologies can be integrated into pre-existing healthcare systems (Jiang et al., 2022).

Expanding markets and technology readiness play crucial roles in the impact digitalization can have on healthcare technology entrepreneurship (Jafari-Sadeghi et al., 2021). Developing economies are compelled to foster environments where digital innovation can thrive in order to take advantage of the benefits of healthcare technology entrepreneurship and technological market expansion (Preko et al., 2020). Telepresence robots in healthcare were one of the first applications of healthcare technology in developing countries, which proved crucial in addressing challenges posed by the COVID-19 pandemic (Wang et al., 2021). Such a use case proved the practical application of healthcare technology entrepreneurship in serving the particular healthcare needs of patients in low-resource settings (Wang et al., 2021).

Yeganegi et al. (2021) analyzed the role of information availability in technology entrepreneurship, noting how innovation in the healthcare sector of developing economies requires high-quality, accessible data. The implications of Big Data in healthcare digitization are far-reaching, with Healthcare 4.0 being an emerging topic in the scholarly research literature (Juneja et al., 2020). Developing economies can use Big Data to vastly improve healthcare outcomes and service delivery (Sharma & Kshetri, 2020). In the long run, healthcare outcomes in developing economies can be improved through research and development, increased funding, renewed policies and public and private support for healthcare innovations and healthcare technology entrepreneurship (Tarkkala et al., 2019).

Biography and Developmental Background of the Protagonists

Pritam Dhalla, a passionate leader and innovator in the healthcare sector, currently steers Larkai Healthcare as its founder. His journey began in 2013, fueled by a burning desire to make healthcare accessible to all. While pursuing his Bachelor's in Technology and Master's in Biotechnology, which he completed in 2018, this vision grew stronger. He was joined by Abhilash Chakraverty, who had leadership roles in Philips Eindhoven Nederlands and GE in Milwaukee, USA, and has worked across the globe. He infused Larkai Healthcare with innovative and diverse healthcare solutions, solidifying its unique position in the industry. His global outlook significantly shaped his approach, seamlessly blending scientific rigor with a deep understanding of real-world healthcare needs.

Background Information on the Product

Born into a family of doctors, Pritam naturally gravitated toward a career in healthcare. Partnering with his pulmonologist father, he brought to life the company's first device, the CardioMate. This innovative technology could detect heart and lung sounds, producing a printed ECG report. However, a crucial question arose: who would be their target customers? Cardiologists, pulmonologists or general physicians? The market research revealed a crucial insight: while high-grade doctors preferred specialized devices, a significant segment craved multifunctionality. They desired ECG alongside capabilities like blood pressure or SpO2 (oxygen saturation) monitoring. This realization sowed the seeds for the WREN, a device designed to cater to this broader market demand.

Keenly observant of market demands and the usual problems faced by ordinary people, Pritam envisioned a solution that was both advanced and accessible to all. WREN, the world's smartest multiparameter portable device, was born from this vision. It seamlessly measured five vital signs: ECG, SpO2, body temperature, NIBP and respiratory rate. WREN transcended a simple device; it is a complete ecosystem, seamlessly connecting with an app and a cloud system for comprehensive health monitoring. While CardioMate held a special place in Pritam's heart, it was commercially a failure. In early 2022, Abhilash, who had two decades of experience in global healthcare giants like Philips and GE, joined him as co-founder and pivoted the company product and market access strategy. Whereas CardioMate was meant for rural low-resource and primary care, WREN resonated with the market's needs. Widely embraced and cherished, WREN has experienced an impressive global expansion, reaching new corners of the world.

The goal of Larkai Healthcare is to use artificial intelligence (AI) in healthcare so that people can receive medical diagnosis and treatment from any location at any time. With its cutting-edge AI technology, the company aims to bridge the gap between diagnosis and treatment by providing immediate and accurate diagnosis. This goal is in line with a larger industry trend that uses AI to improve the effectiveness and accessibility of medical services.

About WREN: Bridging the Gap between Diagnosis and Treatment

Larkai Healthcare's WREN is not aiming to replace traditional ECG monitors in hospitals. Instead, it fills a crucial gap in the healthcare landscape by offering real-time patient monitoring through an advanced, affordable and accessible solution. Bulky ECG machines, while powerful diagnostic tools, lack portability and are often absent from smaller healthcare facilities like nursing homes and clinics.

WREN, in contrast, is a smart, portable multiparameter monitor equipped with a touchscreen, a dedicated app and a cloud system, creating a complete patient monitoring ecosystem. This compact device offers a significant advantage over traditional ECGs:

- **Portability:** WREN's small size (380 grams) and wireless connectivity make it ideal for use in ambulances, nursing homes and even patients' homes. This versatility allows for continuous monitoring during transport and in settings where bulky equipment is impractical.

- **Cost-effectiveness:** Compared to traditional ECG machines, WREN is significantly more affordable ($550 versus $2,200), making it accessible to a wider range of patients and healthcare providers.
- **Real-time monitoring:** WREN's cloud-based system provides doctors with immediate access to patient vitals, enabling them to make informed decisions and adjustments to treatment plans in real time, even remotely.

These features combined made WREN a game-changer in the healthcare market in 2022. Its impact can be seen in:

- **Improved patient care:** WREN's real-time monitoring capabilities allow for earlier detection of potential complications and quicker response times, which leads to improved patient outcomes.
- **Increased access to care:** WREN's affordability and portability make it accessible to underserved communities and patients who might not have access to traditional ECG monitoring.
- **Enhanced healthcare efficiency:** WREN's ability to streamline patient-monitoring processes can save healthcare providers valuable time and resources.

Overall, WREN represented a significant step forward in patient-monitoring technology. It had the potential to revolutionize healthcare delivery and improve patient care for all by bridging the gap between diagnosis and treatment.

Larkai: Company History and Profile

The spark of inspiration struck Pritam back in 2014, during his university days, fueled by the "fail fast, grow early" mantra and the continuous inspiration and enthusiasm instilled by one of his KIIT (Kalinga Institute of Industrial Technology) professors. Embracing the philosophy of "read, learn, launch", Pritam dove headfirst into the world of code, learning to interpret the intricate language of ECG graphs and their peaks. By the end of his fourth year, in 2017, Pritam's brainchild bloomed into existence—his first product, capable of detecting and analyzing heart sounds. This innovation marked a triumphant year, culminating in his first pitch and the subsequent funding for his invention. However, fate threw a curveball. Another company scooped up the idea, forcing Pritam to pivot his design. Instead of viewing this as a setback, Pritam saw an opportunity to innovate. He channeled his creative energy into crafting something even better, something more universally needed—CardioMate. His dedication paid off again in 2019, with CardioMate securing its second round of funding.

Fast forward to 2020, the year Pritam felt the time was ripe to formalize his endeavors. Thus, the seeds of Larkai were sown. On January 1, 2020, Larkai Healthcare officially sprouted, ready to flourish and bear fruit, nurtured by Pritam's unwavering passion and the lessons learned along the way. When the company was initially starting out and had no capital, Larkai Healthcare was able to develop its first product and introduce it to the market with the help of Startup Odisha and the Odisha government (Odisha is a state in Eastern India). This assistance helped the company get traction and caught the attention of investors. Startup Odisha arranged the first pitching, which began late because of some mismanaged planning. Abhilash, the co-founder and director of the company, seized the chance and took the initiative to make the product pitch. He performed an ECG on an investor, Amit Singhal, and other people as soon as he had the opportunity to go center-stage. He presented his idea to five investors, one of whom was Mr. Amit Singhal from Realtime Angel Funds, who was enthralled with the technology and concept of WREN, and this marked the first funding for WREN.

Thus, the company has raised finances from venture capital firms, angel funds and international market funds, in that order. The startup began with a modest proposal to angel investors, and, now, it has a healthy cash chest of millions of dollars. FAAD Network, a significant backer of Larkai Healthcare's seed round, focuses on early-stage investments in a range of industries and regions. Their calculated investment in Larkai Healthcare demonstrates their belief in the company's ability to transform the medical technology industry. More government funds supported Larkai Healthcare's seed funding round in addition to private investments. This cooperative strategy showed a more thorough understanding of the company's possible influence on the healthcare environment.

The Protagonist's Dilemma—Balancing Local and Global Aspirations

Larkai Healthcare leverages cutting-edge solutions to bridge the gap between diagnosis and treatment. However, Larkai's startup status and global aspirations present a unique challenge: keeping pace with global trends while adapting to the Indian market's specific needs. Is it possible for Larkai to balance its goal of helping underprivileged areas in India with its quick worldwide expansion? How can they enter profitable markets while making sure their solutions are still available?

In the fast-paced world of innovation, ideas are fluid, and the first to market often secures the strongest foothold. To achieve global prominence, Larkai must work smart and hard, pioneering solutions for both India and the wider world. How can Larkai strike a balance between innovation and navigability? High-end solutions offer a tempting springboard into lucrative developed markets, accelerating Larkai's global expansion and brand recognition.

Nevertheless, venturing across borders is not without hurdles. Each country's regulatory landscape features distinct approval processes involving lengthy clinical trials, data analysis and safety assessments. These processes can be expensive, time-consuming and prone to unforeseen complications. Moreover, regulatory requirements vary significantly, forcing Larkai to adapt their solutions and evidence to each specific standard—a resource-intensive and potentially frustrating endeavor. Furthermore, even with meticulous preparation, there is no guarantee of approval, leading to delays, additional costs and potentially scrapped projects.

Despite these challenges, the potential rewards are substantial. Being the first mover with a groundbreaking solution can solidify Larkai's position as a med-tech leader and offer previously unmet healthcare solutions, improving patient outcomes and generating significant demand. Is it crucial for Larkai to be the first in every market with new solutions, or could learning from competitors' successes and failures inform a more strategic approach? Larkai's journey demands a delicate balancing act: innovating rapidly while navigating complex regulations. Through careful planning, strategic partnerships and a data-driven approach, they can bridge the gap between their local and global aspirations, securing their place at the forefront of healthcare innovation.

Conclusion—Larkai's Healthcare Innovation with Social Impact

Larkai Healthcare Private Limited has established challenging yet purpose-driven objectives to make a long-lasting impression on the connection between technology and healthcare. The short-term goal of building a strong IT team complements the bigger vision of making healthcare accessible globally. A comprehensive approach to business, where success can be measured not just in financial gains but also in societal and environmental benefits, is underscored by Larkai's dedication to the 3 Ps: Purpose, Profit and Planet.

Larkai's purpose in bridging the gap between technology and healthcare is driven by the company's ambitious goal of impacting 10 million lives by the end of 2024 and 100 million lives in the next two years. This commitment positions Larkai as a transformative force in the global healthcare landscape, striving for positive change. On the profit front, the established revenue goals of $10 million by the end of 2024, followed by a 10x increase to $100 million over the next three years, show a strategic business plan.

Larkai succeeded in securing enough funding to invest in scaling their operations, securing an investment of 500,000 USD for the seed funding round from FAAD Network, QI Ventures, RTAF and additional government grants. Larkai also continues to be recognized and lauded in the business, healthcare and technology communities, receiving many product innovation awards for WREN. The company was recognized as one of the top three finalists in the category of Innovative Diagnostic Solutions for the Aegis Graham Bell Awards for WREN.

Larkai seeks to demonstrate that social responsibility and financial success can be strengthened when combined in the same venture. Larkai is dedicated to reusing, replenishing, refurbishing and recycling, which promotes responsible consumption and is in line with environmental aims. Allowing returns of the product after five years is an inventive way to demonstrate environmentally conscious thinking. Moreover, Larkai incorporates sustainability into all aspects of its business operations, from cutting back on paper usage to using digital substitutes like electronic cards and brochures. Their commitment to environmental preservation is further demonstrated by the recycled materials and non-hazardous materials used in the creation of their products. In 2023, Larkai Healthcare was awarded the GCPIT Global

Sustainability Award 2023 for designing and building sustainable, green medical products that limit hazardous substances, minimize wastage and champion the circular economy.

Last but not least, Larkai's emphasis on diversity and inclusion, as indicated by achieving an equal male-female ratio and receiving workplace excellence awards, demonstrates its dedication to building an inclusive and innovative workplace. Larkai Healthcare Private Limited emerges as a pathfinder in a new era of business, where purpose, profit and the planet combine to create a model of success that is not only financially rewarding but also socially responsible and environmentally sustainable. Their journey sets a notable example for the industry, showcasing that a purpose-driven approach can lead to both business success and positive global impact.

Larkai Healthcare's disruptive innovation with WREN and Bluetail significantly advances patient monitoring and diagnostics, yet challenges persist in making these technologies accessible to the broader population. As a B2B company, Larkai primarily interfaces with healthcare providers and institutions, which poses a barrier to direct access for the general population, particularly in areas where poverty prevails. Despite the strides made, there is a recognition of the need to address this accessibility gap. Larkai is committed to overcoming this disparity by exploring the development of a more accessible lite version of WREN, aligning with their dedication to inclusivity and their mission to bridge the healthcare divide in economically challenged regions.

Acknowledgements

The authors would like to thank Abhilash Chakraverty for providing information for use in this case study.

References

Cozzolino, A. & Geiger, S. (2024). Ecosystem disruption and regulatory positioning: Entry strategies of digital health startup orchestrators and complementors. *Research Policy*, *53*(2), Article 104913. https://doi.org/10.1016/j.respol.2023.104913

Jafari-Sadeghi, V., Garcia-Perez, A., Candelo, E., & Couturier, J. (2021). Exploring the impact of digital transformation on technology entrepreneurship and technological market expansion: The role of technology readiness, exploration and exploitation. *Journal of Business Research*, *124*, 100–111. https://doi.org/10.1016/j.jbusres.2020.11.020

Jiang, C., Chang, H., & Shahzad, I. (2022). Digital economy and health: Does green technology matter in BRICS economies? *Frontiers in Public Health*, *9*, Article 827915. https://doi.org/10.3389/fpubh.2021.827915

Juneja, S., Juneja, A., & Anand, R. (2020). Healthcare 4.0-Digitizing healthcare using big data for performance improvisation. *Journal of Computational and Theoretical Nanoscience*, *17*(9–10), 4408–4410. https://doi.org/10.1166/jctn.2020.9087

Kulkova, J., Kulkov, I., Rohrbeck, R., Lu, S., Khwaja, A., Karjaluoto, H., & Mero, J. (2023). Medicine of the future: How and who is going to treat us? *Futures*, *146*, Article 103097. https://doi.org/10.1016/j.futures.2023.103097

Lee, D. & Yoon, S. N. (2021). Application of artificial intelligence-based technologies in the healthcare industry: Opportunities and challenges. *International Journal of Environmental Research and Public Health*, *18*(1), Article 271. https://doi.org/10.3390/ijerph18010271

Mathur, S. & Sutton, J. (2017). Personalized medicine could transform healthcare. *Biomedical Reports*, *7*(1), 3–5. https://doi.org/10.3892/br.2017.922

Preko, M., Osei-Boateng, R., & Durosinmi, A. E. (2020). Digitalising healthcare in developing economies: Challenges and mitigating strategies. In R. Boateng (Ed.), *Handbook of research on managing information systems in developing economies* (pp. 332–353). IGI Global.

Sharma, R. & Kshetri, N. (2020). Digital healthcare: Historical development, applications, and future research directions. *International Journal of Information Management*, *53*, Article 102105. https://doi.org/10.1016/j.ijinfomgt.2020.102105

Tarkkala, H., Helén, I., & Snell, K. (2019). From health to wealth: The future of personalized medicine in the making. *Futures*, *109*, 142–152. https://doi.org/10.1016/j.futures.2018.06.004

Tortorella, G. L., Fogliatto, F. S., Espôsto, K. F., Mac Cawley, A. F., Vassolo, R., Tlapa, D., & Narayanamurthy, G. (2022). Healthcare costs' reduction through the integration of Healthcare 4.0 technologies in developing economies. *Total Quality Management & Business Excellence*, *33*(3–4), 467–487. https://doi.org/10.1080/14783363.2020.1861934

Wang, M., Pan, C., & Ray, P. K. (2021). Technology entrepreneurship in developing countries: Role of telepresence robots in healthcare. *IEEE Engineering Management Review*, *49*(1), 20–26. https://doi.org/10.1109/EMR.2021.3053258

Yeganegi, S., Laplume, A. O., & Dass, P. (2021). The role of information availability: A longitudinal analysis of technology entrepreneurship.

Technological Forecasting and Social Change, *170*, Article 120910. https://doi.org/10.1016/j.techfore.2021.120910

Supplementary Materials and Further Reading

Bueno, H. & Pérez-Gómez, B. (2019). Global Rounds. *Circulation*, *140*(1), 13–15. https://doi.org/10.1161/circulationaha.119.038714

Crunchbase. (2024). *Larkai Healthcare*. Retrieved April 29, 2024, from www.crunchbase.com/organization/larkai-healthcare

Emilsson, M., Ernstson, U., Gustavsson, L., & Svensson, A. (2020). Sustainable innovations in small enterprises for the transformation of the primary healthcare sector. *Sustainability*, *12*(16), 6391.

Flessa, S. & Huebner, C. (2021). Innovations in health care—A conceptual framework. *International Journal of Environmental Research and Public Health*, *18*(19), Article 10026.

Kulkov, I. (2023). Next-generation business models for artificial intelligence start-ups in the healthcare industry. *International Journal of Entrepreneurial Behavior & Research*, *29*(4), 860–885.

Larkai Healthcare Website. (https://larkai.in).

Larkai Healthcare. (2024). *Larkai Healthcare pitch deck* (confidential).

Ravindranath, M. (2024, February 20). *As regulators play catch up with AI, tech startups say uncertainty is slowing them down*. STAT. www.statnews.com/2024/02/20/health-ai-regulation-tech-startups-compliance/

Vardhan, G. (2024, January 3). *Larkai Healthcare raises $500k in seed round*. EnTrackr. https://entrackr.com/2024/01/larkai-healthcare-raises-500k-in-seed-round/

6 Ivory Coast: Djamo

Bridging the Financial Divide in Francophone Africa

Jordi Diaz, Ray Sanders Muhammad and Tatiana Harkiolakis

Hassan Bourgi, a seasoned entrepreneur, returned to his native Ivory Coast in 2019 after selling his first startup, Busportal, to Naspers. He has a vision to revolutionize the financial landscape. Witnessing the frustration of millennials with traditional banking experiences, Bourgi partnered with Régis Bamba, a telecoms veteran, to launch Djamo in Abidjan, Ivory Coast. Djamo's mission is to bridge the vast gap in financial inclusion for Francophone Africa, where a mere 25% of adults hold bank accounts. Traditional banks cater to a select few, leaving the remaining 120 million unbanked and underserved.

Here's where Djamo steps in—leveraging mobile money infrastructure, which is prevalent in the region, to offer seamless and affordable banking solutions. Bourgi's prior experience building mass-market consumer products proved invaluable. Djamo prioritized a user-friendly mobile platform, in stark contrast to the cumbersome in-person banking prevalent then. This focus on a superior user experience, alongside faster customer service, resonated with the tech-savvy millennial generation.

Understanding the diverse needs within this sizeable unbanked population, Djamo avoids a one-size-fits-all approach. Whether it's facilitating online payments or providing readily available Visa debit cards, Djamo tailors its offerings to specific user segments. This approach, coupled with positive word-of-mouth, has fueled Djamo's organic growth.

Djamo stands out by prioritizing affordability. Unlike traditional banks, Djamo offers zero-fee cards with a pay-as-you-go transaction model. They even have a premium plan with higher limits for a minimal monthly fee. Within a short period of its 2019 launch, Djamo

DOI: 10.4324/9781003616108-6

has amassed over 90,000 registered users and processes 50,000 transactions monthly. However, this success came with its challenges. Unlike established payment ecosystems in other African regions, Ivory Coast lacked reliable infrastructure providers. Djamo's resourcefulness shone through as they navigated between different providers to ensure smooth operations. Security concerns, a common hurdle for new fintech startups (Diallo et al., 2024; Tompihe, 2023), were addressed by Bourgi and Bamba through robust onboarding, KYC (Know Your Customer) processes and secure transaction systems. Delivering Visa cards presented another obstacle. The lack of efficient logistics services in Ivory Coast prompted Djamo to develop an in-house delivery app with dedicated agents, ensuring timely card delivery to their customers.

Even before launching their minimum viable product (MVP), Djamo secured a pre-seed investment of $350,000—a record for the Francophone region. This funding, coupled with the founders' track record, validated Djamo's innovative approach. For a long time, investors have overlooked Francophone Africa. However, the region boasts a burgeoning startup scene and holds immense potential (Aker, 2022).

With Djamo being the first Y Combinator-backed fintech startup from the region, it signifies a shift in investor focus toward this promising market (Kene-Okafor, 2021). The startup has processed more than $4.5 billion in transactions since it was launched (Kene-Okafor, 2025). Régis Bamba, Chief Product Officer and Co-Founder, stated that the startup's primary growth has been organic, driven by word-of-mouth referrals. He further indicated a commitment to ensuring optimal user value (Nwokoma, 2022). Djamo's success story exemplifies the immense opportunity for disruption in under-represented regions like Francophone Africa. Their user-centric approach, focus on affordability and commitment to security are paving the way for a more inclusive financial future for millions (Kamau, 2022).

Background Information on Fintech and Banking in Africa

The enduring challenge of financial inclusion, defined as the equitable access to and utilization of affordable and appropriate financial products and services, remains a salient issue within developing economies (Ahmed et al., 2024). The inherent limitations in the operational scope and infrastructural capacity of traditional banking systems frequently result in the exclusion of a substantial segment of the population, leaving them unbanked and underserved (Sanga & Aziakpono, 2024). This phenomenon is particularly pronounced and multifaceted within the context of Francophone Africa, where a confluence of distinct historical, socio-economic and institutional conditions exacerbates the existing difficulties in fostering widespread financial participation (Aker, 2022).

The legacy of colonial-era financial architectures, often designed to facilitate the economic interests of the metropole rather than the needs of the indigenous populations, continues to shape the financial landscape of many Francophone African nations (Séraphin, 2024). This has resulted in a system that may not adequately cater to the diverse economic activities and income levels prevalent in these societies. Furthermore, lower levels of economic development, coupled with infrastructural deficits, particularly in rural and remote areas, impede the physical expansion of traditional banking networks (Aker, 2022). This geographical constraint directly limits access for a significant portion of the population, increasing the costs and complexities associated with accessing formal financial services. The interplay of these factors creates a unique and challenging environment for advancing financial inclusion within the Francophone African context, demanding nuanced and context-specific interventions (Séraphin, 2024).

Financial Infrastructure: A Significant Hurdle

The significant divergence between economies predominantly reliant on cash transactions and those increasingly embracing digital financial systems constitutes a considerable obstacle to the advancement of financial inclusion within developing nations (Ahmed et al., 2024). While regions such as Europe have witnessed a widespread transition toward cashless modalities, numerous African states, particularly those situated outside the West African Monetary Institute (WAMI) economic sphere, demonstrate a persistent and substantial dependence on physical currency (Avom et al., 2023). This deeply rooted reliance on cash introduces complexities into the implementation of digital transformation initiatives, thereby necessitating the formulation of context-sensitive strategies tailored to the specific characteristics of diverse regional contexts. Consequently, effectively addressing these fundamental disparities demands a meticulously calibrated and nuanced approach that duly considers the idiosyncratic needs and existing infrastructural frameworks of individual countries (Callice, 2024).

Beyond the demonstrable limitations in established financial infrastructure, developing countries are confronted with a multiplicity of additional impediments in their pursuit of comprehensive financial inclusion (Aker, 2022). The geographically constrained presence of physical bank branches, particularly within rural and underserved areas, renders traditional banking services both inaccessible and economically prohibitive for a considerable segment of the population (Chikweche et al., 2024). Illustratively, the case of Ivory Coast highlights the critical role of robust payment infrastructure; the absence thereof, in stark contrast to Nigeria's well-established digital payment platforms such as Flutterwave and Paystack, compels nascent financial technology companies like Djamo to navigate operational challenges arising from reliance on less dependable service providers (Demirgüç-Kunt et al., 2022).

Furthermore, the operational modalities of conventional banking services often present inherent barriers to accessibility for low-income populations (Ndung'u, 2022). The imposition of substantial account maintenance fees, stringent minimum balance requirements and the provision of costly loan alternatives serve to further impede the financial inclusion of these demographics (Avom et al., 2023). Concurrently, a prevalent lack of adequate financial literacy among individuals hinders their capacity to comprehend and effectively utilize the available, albeit often inaccessible, financial products and services (Demirgüç-Kunt et al., 2022).

Moreover, the significant proportion of the workforce engaged in the informal economic sector across many developing countries encounters considerable difficulties in accessing formal financial services due to the absence of standardized documentation or a consistent and verifiable income stream (International Labour Organization, 2018). The overall customer experience associated with traditional banking in these contexts is frequently characterized by inefficiencies, including protracted wait times, restrictive operating hours, unreliable mobile banking applications and inadequate levels of customer support (Demirgüç-Kunt & Klapper, 2012). These cumulative factors contribute to notably diminished Net Promoter Scores (NPS), serving as a quantifiable indicator of widespread customer dissatisfaction (NPS Prism, 2024).

The Francophone Africa Context

Francophone Africa presents a unique and compelling context for the study of financial technology innovation (Nwokoma, 2022). The historical trajectory of the region, marked by comparatively lower levels of international investment, has resulted in it often being overshadowed by its Anglophone counterparts in key economic indicators such as aggregate economic growth, gross domestic product and the influx of venture capital funding (Séraphin, 2024). These economic realities, when coupled with the inherent complexities arising from diverse linguistic landscapes, have collectively contributed to the evolution of a financial ecosystem that, until recently, lagged behind in terms of development and sophistication (Demirgüç-Kunt et al., 2022).

The foundational structures of the financial system in Francophone Africa bear the indelible imprint of its colonial past (Tompihe, 2023). The inherited banking infrastructure was predominantly oriented toward facilitating the economic objectives of the former colonial powers, often at the expense of adequately addressing the nuanced financial requirements of the local populations (Demirgüç-Kunt & Klapper, 2012). This historical alignment has contributed to a system that may not be optimally suited to the socio-economic realities and diverse income strata prevalent across the region (Séraphin, 2024).

Furthermore, Francophone African nations have a generally lower gross domestic product and per capita income in contrast to their Anglophone counterparts (Séraphin, 2024). These factors have historically rendered investments in expansive financial infrastructure less financially appealing to conventional banking institutions (Demirgüç-Kunt et al., 2022). Consequently, with a significant majority of the adult population (over 75%) remaining unbanked, traditional financial entities have predominantly focused on serving a limited segment of the population, typically the wealthiest 10–20%, while overlooking the considerable unbanked demographic (estimated at around 120 million) deemed to be of insufficient profitability (Kene-Okafor, 2021).

However, the established paradigm began to undergo a notable transformation around the year 2019. The Francophone African region commenced a period of accelerated economic expansion, with expert forecasts suggesting its increasing contribution to the continent's most rapidly growing economies (Bughin et al., 2016). This burgeoning economic dynamism progressively captured the attention of international investors, who increasingly recognized the substantial, yet previously underexploited, potential inherent within these markets (Séraphin, 2024). While the quantum of investment directed toward Francophone African startups remained comparatively modest in relation to the levels observed in Anglophone Africa, the emergence and early successes of prominent ventures such as Oolu and Healthlane, both of which received backing from the prestigious Y Combinator accelerator, served as tangible indicators of a nascent yet significant surge in investor interest and confidence (Kene-Okafor, 2021). This shift signals a potentially transformative period for fintech innovation within the region.

Emerging Solutions

Despite the enduring and multifaceted challenges impeding financial inclusion across developing nations, a significant and transformative wave of innovation is actively reshaping the financial services landscape, with notable implications for Francophone Africa (Séraphin, 2024). The proliferation of mobile money services, spearheaded by telecommunications operators, has fundamentally democratized access to basic financial functionalities throughout the African continent (Akinyosoye–Gbonda & Kamara, 2024). These platforms empower individuals to engage in essential financial activities such as storing and transferring monetary value, facilitating bill payments and even accessing microcredit facilities, all through the ubiquitous medium of their mobile telephones (Mpofu, 2023).

The widespread adoption is evident in countries like Ivory Coast, where a substantial 83% of the population actively utilizes mobile money platforms (Nwokoma, 2022). However, while undeniably a groundbreaking innovation, the primary utility of mobile money remains largely concentrated within a specific segment of the user base, primarily catering to basic transactional needs (Avom et al., 2023). The middle and upper echelons of the financial hierarchy increasingly demand and seek more sophisticated and comprehensive financial product offerings that extend beyond rudimentary local transfers and utility bill settlements (GSM Association [GSMA], 2023).

Concurrently, the Francophone African region is witnessing the emergence of a burgeoning ecosystem of financial technology startups. These nascent enterprises are at the forefront of developing and deploying novel and user-centric financial products meticulously tailored to address the specific needs and circumstances of the substantial unbanked and underbanked segments of the population (Etudaiye-Muhtar et al., 2024). These agile ventures strategically leverage advancements in digital technologies to effectively circumvent the traditional barriers that have historically impeded financial inclusion, thereby delivering more accessible and inclusive financial services.

The implementation of agent banking models, which strategically utilize existing retail infrastructure such as local shops and kiosks, plays a crucial role in extending the reach of fundamental financial services into geographically remote and underserved localities (Sanga & Aziakpono, 2024). This innovative approach significantly enhances accessibility while simultaneously mitigating the substantial capital expenditure associated with establishing and maintaining traditional brick-and-mortar bank branches (Demirgüç-Kunt et al., 2022).

In conclusion, the pursuit of comprehensive financial inclusion in developing countries, with a particular emphasis on the unique context of Francophone Africa, remains an ongoing and dynamic process (Tompihe, 2023). Sustained advancements in mobile communication technologies, the establishment of enabling and supportive regulatory frameworks conducive to financial technology innovation and the implementation of robust financial literacy initiatives are indispensable prerequisites for achieving a further broadening of access to essential financial services across the region (Séraphin, 2024). The success story of financial technology startups like Djamo aptly exemplifies their pivotal role in dismantling long-standing traditional impediments and delivering user-centric financial solutions to a significant portion of the population (Kene-Okafor, 2025).

Djamo's strategic approach encompasses many innovative aspects (Kene-Okafor, 2025). These aspects include the leveraging of existing mobile money infrastructure, the implementation of an innovative freemium business model and the cultivation of strategic partnerships with both local financial institutions and prominent international organizations such as Visa, powerfully underscoring the transformative potential of financial technology innovation in driving meaningful financial inclusion (Kene-Okafor, 2021). Ultimately, through concerted and collaborative efforts involving governments, established financial institutions and agile financial technology companies, the considerable potential for a more inclusive and economically vibrant future for Francophone Africa can be effectively realized (Mpofu, 2023).

Hassan Bourgi: A Visionary Leader for Francophone Africa's Fintech Future

Hassan Bourgi's entrepreneurial journey reflects a global outlook and a passion for identifying and solving problems in underserved markets. Hailing from Lebanon, Hassan's academic background is a testament to his dedication to business and finance. His Bachelor's in Business Administration from MBS (Montpellier), with an exchange program at Melbourne's La Trobe University, broadened his perspective on international business. He further honed his expertise with a Master's in Management from EADA (2010–2011) and a Master's in Finance from Universidad del CEMA (Buenos Aires).

Hassan's early career experience exposed him to diverse business environments. Internship stints at HSBC Private Bank and Think Great Consulting laid the groundwork for his entrepreneurial pursuits. In 2012, he co-founded Busportal with Carol Riboud, seizing a business opportunity in Peru's underserved online bus ticketing market. Their success culminated in a lucrative acquisition by Redbus (Naspers) in 2016, marking a 5x increase in valuation (SemanaEconomica, n.d.).

This accomplishment fueled Hassan's desire to create an even greater impact. Busportal achieved significant success, and Hassan realized the importance of building a product that is deeply integrated into people's daily lives. This crucial insight became a cornerstone for the creation of Djamo. Returning to his native Ivory Coast, he met Régis Bamba, a seasoned telecommunications professional with MTN. Together, their shared vision of financial inclusion for Francophone Africa led to the birth of Djamo. Hassan's leadership, combined with his international business acumen and financial expertise, positions him perfectly to guide Djamo in its mission to revolutionize the financial landscape for millions in Francophone Africa.

Leveraging Technology to Transform Financial Services

Francophone Africa has long been underserved by traditional banking institutions. Complex regulatory landscapes, limited financial infrastructure and a largely unbanked population have created a significant gap in the market. Djamo emerged to challenge the status quo, offering a fresh approach to financial services that was tailored to the unique needs of the region. At the heart of Djamo's proposition is its Visa card, a product that has redefined access to financial services for millions. Obtaining a Visa card is typically a complex process, requiring regulatory approvals, partnerships with local banks and adherence to stringent international standards.

Djamo's success in navigating this intricate landscape is a testament to its ability to overcome hurdles and deliver innovative solutions. By partnering with local banks, Djamo has been able to issue "local" cards, which are crucial for ensuring widespread acceptance by merchants. This strategic decision, coupled with the company's focus on regulatory compliance, has been instrumental in building trust with both customers and financial institutions. Djamo's mobile app is the cornerstone of its customer experience. The app is designed with simplicity and accessibility in mind, empowering users to manage their finances effortlessly. From opening accounts and transferring funds to paying bills and topping up mobile airtime, the app streamlines everyday banking tasks. By eliminating the need for physical branches and reducing reliance on paper-based transactions, Djamo is driving financial inclusion and empowering individuals to take control of their financial lives.

To democratize access to financial services, Djamo employs a freemium model. Basic banking services, such as account management and money transfers, are offered free of charge. For users requiring advanced features like priority customer support, higher transaction limits and additional perks, a premium subscription is available for a nominal fee of 2,000 F CFA, around 3€ monthly. This approach not only attracts a wider customer base but also encourages deeper engagement with the platform. Djamo's revenue model is two-fold. The core revenue stream comes from interchange fees charged to merchants for processing transactions made with Djamo cards. This revenue stream aligns the company's interests with increased card usage, incentivizing product adoption and driving customer acquisition. Subscription fees from premium users provide an additional revenue source.

Security is paramount in the digital age. Djamo prioritizes robust security measures, including secure onboarding processes, rigorous Know Your Customer (KYC) verification and advanced fraud prevention technologies. By safeguarding user data and funds, Djamo builds trust and fosters long-term customer relationships. Furthermore, Djamo's focus on seamless online payments is a game-changer. By enabling users to make purchases on global platforms like Alibaba,

Amazon and Netflix, the company is connecting Francophone Africa to the digital economy. This development is particularly significant given the region's previously limited access to international online services.

Djamo's commitment to exceptional customer service is evident in its efficient support channels and rapid response times. By addressing customer needs promptly and effectively, the company builds loyalty and fosters positive word-of-mouth. In conclusion, Djamo's innovative approach to banking has disrupted the traditional financial landscape in Francophone Africa. By combining a user-centric mobile app, accessible fee structures, robust security measures and a focus on financial inclusion, Djamo is empowering individuals and driving economic growth in the region.

Djamo: A Fintech Disruptor Bridging the Financial Gap in Francophone Africa

The Birth of a Fintech Pioneer (2019)

Djamo, a revolutionary force in Francophone Africa's financial landscape, emerged in 2019. Founded by a dynamic duo—Hassan Bourgi, a seasoned entrepreneur, and Régis Bamba, a telecoms veteran—Djamo was born from a shared vision of financial inclusion. Witnessing the frustration of millennials with traditional banking's limitations, they set out to create a more accessible and user-friendly financial solution. The startup's primary goal was to ensure customers could manage their money correctly.

Djamo's target market was primarily urbanites within the region. It focused on a specific segment: the "bank-ready" population. This group represented an estimated 25 million people in the region who required their first proper bank account. Djamo's decision to target this segment was based on the belief that mobile money solutions already served the needs of the mass market effectively. By focusing on the "bank-ready" population, Djamo aimed to offer a more comprehensive and advanced banking experience. Djamo helped them improve their financial health and better plan their financial future. For example, they have developed vaults, a gamified, social saving option. This placement will clearly define Djamo's customer base and differentiate it from competitors targeting different market segments.

Building Djamo: Overcoming Challenges (2019)

Djamo's journey to becoming a leading fintech player in Francophone Africa has been marked by significant hurdles. The startup's early days were characterized by a series of challenges that required innovative solutions and unwavering determination.

Operational Obstacles

One of the most pressing issues faced by Djamo was the lack of reliable infrastructure. The absence of efficient payment processors and service providers forced the company to adapt and switch between different partners to maintain operations. This agility was crucial in ensuring uninterrupted services for customers. Moreover, gaining the trust of both banks and customers was a formidable challenge. Djamo had to implement robust security measures and transparent processes to dispel skepticism surrounding fintech startups in the region. Rigorous onboarding and KYC procedures were essential to establish credibility and build confidence among users.

Delivering the Promise

Physical delivery of Djamo Visa cards presented another obstacle. Unlike more developed regions, Ivory Coast lacked efficient logistics infrastructure. To overcome this challenge, Djamo developed an in-house delivery app and built a dedicated delivery team. This innovative approach ensured that customers received their cards promptly, enhancing overall customer satisfaction.

Early Validation and Investment

Despite the challenges, Djamo's potential was recognized early on. The startup secured a pre-seed investment of $350,000 in June 2019, a significant achievement for a fintech company in the Francophone region. This funding validated Djamo's business model and provided the necessary resources to fuel growth. The ingenuity of Djamo's solution, coupled with the founders' track record, played a pivotal role in attracting investors. By addressing the specific needs of the unbanked population and offering a user-friendly platform, Djamo positioned itself as a promising disruptor in the African fintech landscape.

A Beacon of Change: First Y Combinator-Backed Fintech Startup (2021)

In 2021, Djamo made history by becoming the first fintech startup from Francophone Africa to be backed by Y Combinator. This landmark achievement marked a pivotal moment, signaling to the global investment community the region's burgeoning potential for financial innovation. With a user base of 90,000 and processing over 50,000 monthly transactions, Djamo's traction was undeniable. Following its successful Y Combinator stint, the company was selected for Visa's Fast Track program, providing a strategic platform to expand its reach and introduce cutting-edge payment solutions.

Fueling Growth: $14 Million Expansion (2022)

Djamo's dedication to its mission has not gone unnoticed. In November 2022, they secured a $14 million funding round from the famed Y Combinator accelerator, as well as from others among the best funds, including Enza Capital, Oikocredit and Partech Africa (Tech Gist Africa, 2022), further propelling their expansion plans across Francophone Africa, starting with Senegal. This investment empowered them to continue developing their financial super app, reaching new markets and empowering millions with financial inclusion. In less than three years, Djamo has become Ivory Coast's leading card issuer, well in front of major banks.

Evolving into a Personal Finance Super App (2023–Present)

In a strategic move to accelerate user acquisition and solidify its position as the primary bank for Africa's digital natives, Djamo introduced a B2B2C product focused on salary payments in 2023. This innovative solution allows businesses to seamlessly pay salaries directly into Djamo accounts, encouraging employees to open accounts and experience the platform's benefits firsthand. By becoming the preferred destination for salary deposits, Djamo aims to deepen its relationship with customers and foster long-term loyalty. This expansion into the B2B space marks a significant milestone in Djamo's journey to revolutionize the financial landscape in Francophone Africa.

Djamo's journey continues to evolve. The company is strategically expanding its offerings beyond core banking services. They are transforming into a personal finance super app, offering additional functionalities to cater to the diverse needs of their user base (Jackson, 2023). This strategic shift positions Djamo to become a one-stop solution for managing finances in Francophone Africa. People see more and more value in Djamo's product as they add features, which is reflected in our high percentage of paid subscribers. All of this allowed the company to have a double-digit monthly revenue growth over the last 12 months.

Currently, Djamo boasts a growing user base of 750,000 active users, with a substantial portion as paid subscribers contributing to an annual revenue, in 2023, of 16 million. This impressive figure is primarily driven by transaction fees, accounting for 75% of total revenue. Subscription plans contribute an additional 15%, while card issuing and lending services generate the remaining 10%. The platform's user base is composed of 40% banked users who primarily use the platform for convenience and reliability, 40% bank-ready users seeking a full-fledged banking solution and 10% professionals utilizing Djamo for small business financial management. This diverse user base underscores Djamo's potential to capture a significant market share and solidify its position as a leading financial technology provider in the region.

The Road Ahead: A More Inclusive Financial Future

With a growing user base, a commitment to continuous improvement and a focus on affordability and user experience, Djamo is well-positioned to become a leading financial super app. Their dedication to financial inclusion paves the way for a more empowered and financially secure future for millions in Francophone Africa. Djamo's story serves as a testament to the transformative power of innovation in underserved markets, inspiring a wave of change across the continent.

Djamo: A Vision for the Future

Djamo's success thus far is a testament to its ability to identify and address the specific needs of the Francophone African market. Djamo operates today in Ivory Coast and Senegal. As the company continues to grow, several key areas of focus will be crucial for sustained success.

Expanding Product Offerings and Financial Services

To drive sustained growth, Djamo must continually innovate and expand its product offerings. The lending market presents a significant opportunity, given the limited access to loans in Africa, limited to 5% of the population. By offering short-term, unsecured loans tailored to the needs of its customer base, Djamo can address a critical gap in the market and generate additional revenue streams.

Expanding into investment products, such as mutual funds, can also contribute to customer satisfaction and loyalty. While the current investment landscape in Africa is relatively underdeveloped, there is potential for growth as investor sophistication increases. Today, they are offering mutual funds, very low-risk instruments, with 7–8% of annual interest. By offering a diversified range of financial products, Djamo can position itself as a one-stop financial solution for its customers.

Geographical Expansion and Market Penetration

Djamo's decision to prioritize geographical expansion is strategic. By diversifying its market presence, the company can mitigate risks associated with operating in individual countries. With a focus on replicating the success achieved in Ivory Coast and Senegal, Djamo is poised to expand its footprint within the WAEMU region because of its potential target segment growth.

However, replicating success will require a deep understanding of local market dynamics and customer preferences within each country. While the Nubank-in-Brazil model is inspiring, it's essential to recognize the unique challenges and opportunities presented by the African market. A tailored approach that combines the best practices of global fintech leaders with a deep understanding of local context will be crucial for long-term success.

Strengthening Partnerships and Building an Ecosystem

Djamo's partnerships with local banks have been instrumental in its growth. Expanding these collaborations and forging new alliances with other financial institutions, telecommunications companies and technology providers will be essential for scaling operations and enhancing the customer experience. By building a robust ecosystem, Djamo can create synergies and unlock new opportunities. For example, partnering with mobile network operators could facilitate customer acquisition and expand product reach.

Government Collaboration and Policy Advocacy

The role of government in fostering a conducive environment for fintech innovation cannot be overstated. Djamo can play a pivotal role in advocating for policies that support financial inclusion, digital infrastructure development and regulatory frameworks that promote innovation. By engaging with policymakers, Djamo can contribute to shaping the future of the fintech industry in Francophone Africa. In conclusion, Djamo is well-positioned to become a leading financial services provider in Francophone Africa. By focusing on product innovation, strategic partnerships and a deep understanding of the local market, the company can continue to disrupt the status quo and improve the financial well-being of millions of people.

Djamo's Next Chapter: Expanding Horizons or Deepening Focus?

Francophone Africa presents a unique tapestry of economic and financial development characterized by stark contrasts and immense potential. While the region has witnessed burgeoning economic growth, the financial landscape remains largely underserved. This disparity has created a fertile ground for innovative solutions, such as Djamo, to emerge and thrive. At the heart of this landscape is a population grappling with limited access to formal financial services. The majority of the population relies on cash-based transactions, with mobile money serving as a partial bridge to the digital economy. A significant portion of the population, however, remains entirely excluded from the formal financial system; this presents a substantial opportunity for financial institutions and fintech companies to tap into an underserved market.

Djamo has carved a niche for itself by targeting the "bank-ready" segment of the population—those with the potential to be the next 30 million banked individuals. These are individuals who have outgrown the limitations of mobile money and are seeking a more comprehensive banking experience. By offering a user-friendly mobile app, accessible fee structures and a Visa card, Djamo has successfully attracted this segment and demonstrated the potential for a scalable business model.

However, the journey ahead is fraught with challenges. The competitive landscape is intensifying, with established players like traditional banks and emerging fintech competitors vying for market share. Wave, a formidable rival, has shown remarkable success in capturing the mobile money market and is poised to expand its offerings. Djamo faces a critical crossroads. Should it deepen its focus on the "bank-ready" segment, refining its product offerings and strengthening its market position? Or should it broaden its target audience to include the underbanked and financially excluded populations? Both paths present significant opportunities and challenges.

Expanding into new segments would require substantial investments in financial education, product development and distribution channels. It would also necessitate navigating complex regulatory environments and building trust in a market with low financial literacy. On the other hand, focusing solely on the "bank-ready" segment risks limiting long-term growth potential as this segment matures. The choice is complex, but Djamo's ability to adapt and innovate will be crucial to its continued success. By leveraging its strong brand, deep understanding of the customer and technological capabilities, Djamo has the potential to become a leading financial services provider in Francophone Africa, driving financial inclusion and empowering millions of people. The road ahead is undoubtedly challenging, but with a clear mission, vision, strategic execution and a relentless focus on customer needs, Djamo can navigate the complexities of the market and emerge as a transformative force in the region's financial landscape.

From Disruption to Dominance: Shaping the Future of African Banking

Djamo emerged as a beacon of hope in a region starved for accessible financial services. With a mission to provide financial inclusion in a region characterized by high rates of financial exclusion and exorbitant fees, Djamo has challenged the status quo and offered innovative solutions tailored to the unique needs of the Francophone African population. The company's journey has been marked by both remarkable achievements and significant challenges. By successfully tapping into the "bank-ready" segment and offering a compelling value proposition, Djamo has established itself as a formidable player in the market. However, the path to sustained growth and expansion is fraught with complexities.

To navigate this dynamic landscape, Djamo must make strategic choices regarding its focus and growth strategy. Should the company deepen its penetration in the "bank-ready" segment or expand its target market to include the underbanked and financially excluded populations? Each path presents unique opportunities and challenges. Geographical expansion, while promising, requires a nuanced understanding of local markets and significant investments in resources and infrastructure. Additionally, the reliance on third-party service providers has exposed Djamo to operational risks and customer dissatisfaction. As Djamo looks to the future, it is imperative to prioritize customer needs, invest in technology and talent and build strategic partnerships. By doing so, the company can position itself as a leading force in the transformation of the African financial landscape.

Acknowledgements

The authors would like to thank Pol Borràs Font for providing background information for use in this case study.

References

Ahmed, J. U., Ahmed, A., Mazid, T. S., & Gani, M. O. (2024). Chari: A FMCG B2B platform with incorporation of Fintech. *Journal of Information Technology Teaching Cases*, *14*(1), 129–133. https://doi.org/10.1177/20438869231163600

Aker, J. C. (2022). Fintech for rural markets in sub-Saharan Africa. In T. Madon, A. J. Gadgil, R. Anderson, & L. Casaburi (Eds.), *Introduction to development engineering: A framework with applications from the field* (pp. 247–268). Springer Cham.

Akinyosoye–Gbonda, O. O. & Kamara, A. (2024). Utilising digital innovation for sustainable development–The case of mobile money in Sierra Leone. *International Journal of Innovation Scientific Research and Review*, *6*(5), 6424–6437. http://journalijisr.com/sites/default/files/issues-pdf/IJISRR-1587.pdf

Avom, D., Bangaké, C., & Ndoya, H. (2023). Do financial innovations improve financial inclusion? Evidence from mobile money adoption in Africa. *Technological Forecasting and Social Change*, *190*, Article 122451. https://doi.org/10.1016/j.techfore.2023.122451

Bughin, J., Chironga, M., Desvaux, G., Ermias, T., Jacobson, P., Kassiri, O., Leke, A., Lund, S., Van Wamelen, A., & Zouaoui, Y. (2016). *Lions on the move II: Realizing the potential of Africa's economies*. McKinsey Global

Institute. www.mckinsey.com/~/media/mckinsey/featured%20insights/middle%20east%20and%20africa/realizing%20the%20potential%20of%20africas%20economies/mgi-lions-on-the-move-2-executive-summary-september-2016v2.pdf

Callice, P. (2024). *Financial sector policy in fragile states: A primer*. World Bank Group. http://documents.worldbank.org/curated/en/099061124042525797

Chikweche, T., Lappeman, J., & Egan, P. (2024). Marketing financial services in Africa: Exploring the heterogeneous middle-class consumer across nine countries. *Journal of Financial Services Marketing, 29*(1), 1–16. https://doi.org/10.1057/s41264-022-00179-4

Demirgüç-Kunt, A., Klapper, L., Singer, D., & Ansar, S. (2022). *The Global Findex Database 2021: Financial inclusion, digital payments, and resilience in the age of COVID-19*. The World Bank. www.worldbank.org/en/publication/globalfindex

Demirgüç-Kunt, A. & Klapper, L. F. (2012). *Financial inclusion in Africa: An overview* (World Bank Policy Research Working Paper No. 6088). https://ssrn.com/abstract=2084599

Diallo, A., Samhi, J., Bissyandé, T., & Klein, J. (2024). *(In) security of mobile apps in developing countries: A systematic literature review*. ArXiv. https://arxiv.org/abs/2405.05117

Etudaiye-Muhtar, F. O., Johan, S., Lawal, R., & Sakariyahu, R. (2024). Fintech, human development and energy poverty in sub-Saharan Africa. *Journal of International Financial Markets, Institutions and Money, 91*, Article 101931. https://doi.org/10.1016/j.intfin.2023.101931

GSM Association. (2023). *The state of the industry report on mobile money in 2023*. www.gsma.com/solutions-and-impact/connectivity-for-good/mobile-for-development/gsma_resources/state-of-the-industry-report-on-mobile-money-2023-2/

International Labour Organization. (2018, April 30). *More than 60 per cent of the world's employed population are in the informal economy*. www.ilo.org/resource/news/more-60-cent-world's-employed-population-are-informal-economy

Jackson, T. (2023, May 19). *How Ivory Coast's Djamo has expanded to become a personal finance super-app*. Disrupt Africa. https://disruptafrica.com/2023/05/19/how-ivory-coasts-djamo-has-expanded-to-become-a-personal-finance-super-app/

Kamau, P. (2022, May 12). *Y Combinator-backed fintech Djamo raises $14m to build a personal finance app in Francophone Africa*. Africa Business Communities. https://africabusinesscommunities.com/tech/tech-news/y-combinator-backed-fintech-djamo-raises-14m-to-build-a-personal-finance-app-in-francophone-africa/

Kene-Okafor, T. (2021, February 5). *YC-backed Djamo is building a financial super app for consumers in Francophone Africa. TechCrunch.* https://techcrunch.com/2021/02/05/yc-backed-djamo-is-building-a-financial-super-app-for-consumers-in-francophone-africa/

Kene-Okafor, T. (2025, April 3). *Y Combinator neobank Djamo raises $17M with 1M users across Francophone Africa. TechCrunch.* https://techcrunch.com/2025/04/03/djamo-raises-17m-and-has-1m-users-across-francophone-africa/

Mpofu, F. Y. (2023). Fintech, the fourth industrial revolution technologies, digital financial services and the advancement of the SDGs in developing countries. *International Journal of Social Science Research and Review, 6*(1), 533–553. https://ijssrr.com/journal/article/view/752

Ndung'u, N. (2022). *Fintech in sub-Saharan Africa* (WIDER Working Paper 2022/101). https://includeplatform.net/wp-content/uploads/2022/10/wp2022-101-fintech-sub-saharan-africa.pdf

NPS Prism. (2024, December 16). *2024 Global Banking NPS Benchmarks Report.* www.npsprism.com/blog/global-banking-nps-benchmarks-2024

Nwokoma, C. (2022, November 24). *Ivorian fintech startup, Djamo, gets $14 million to expand financial services product to Francophone Africa.* Techpoint Africa. https://techpoint.africa/2022/11/24/djamo-14-million-francophone-africa/

Sanga, B. & Aziakpono, M. (2024). FinTech developments and their heterogeneous effect on digital finance for SMEs and entrepreneurship: Evidence from 47 African countries. *Journal of Entrepreneurship in Emerging Economies.* Advance online publication. https://doi.org/10.1108/JEEE-09-2023-0379

SemanaEconomica. (n.d.). *Empresa india Redbus compra mayoría de acciones de Busportal.pe* [Indian company Redbus acquires majority stake in Busportal.pe]. https://semanaeconomica.com/que-esta-pasando/articulos/194187-empresa-india-redbus-compra-mayoria-de-acciones-de-busportal-pe

Séraphin, P. Y. (2024). Financial liberalization and banking risks in the Waemu Zone: Do Fintechs matter? *International Journal of Accounting and Financial Reporting, 14*(2), 25–45. https://doi.org/10.5296/ijafr.v14i2.21990

Tech Gist Africa. (2022, November 28). *Djamo, an African fintech business, has raised $14 million in a funding round.* https://techgistafrica.com/funding/djamo-an-african-fintech-business-has-raised-14-million-in-a-funding-round/

Tompihe, J. G. (2023). Financing terrorism with fintechs in West Africa? In S. Ahmed, J. A. Addae, & K. S. Ofori (Eds.), *Exploring the dark side of fintech and implications of monetary policy* (pp. 118–143). IGI Global. https://doi.org/10.4018/978-1-6684-6381-9.ch006

7 Cyprus: Transforming the Workspace Culture in Cyprus

The Journey of MyOffice Cyprus

Marcos Komodromos and Marios Vassiliou

Coworking spaces are not just about sharing desks; they're about building communities, fostering innovation and redefining the future of work.

Introduction—The Dawn of a New Work Era

In recent years, the coworking space industry has transformed how professionals approach work. It offers flexible, collaborative, cost-effective alternatives to traditional office environments (Robelski et al., 2019). As the gig economy expands and remote work gains popularity, coworking spaces are becoming essential hubs for innovation and community-building. These shared workspaces cater to freelancers, startups, small businesses and large enterprises seeking flexibility (Huang et al., 2020; Kinsman, Marris & Oakman, 2023). The global growth of coworking spaces has been remarkable. By 2024, the number of coworking spaces worldwide had exceeded 21,000. The need for flexible and convenient working setups fuels this growth. These spaces are crucial in nurturing creativity, promoting networking and enabling professionals to expand their businesses without the extended commitments associated with traditional office leases (Wall & Crowe, 2023).

In Cyprus, a country historically reliant on tourism, real estate and shipping industries, the emergence of digital entrepreneurship and the startup ecosystem has created a demand for modern, flexible workspaces. The growth of sectors like information and communication technology (ICT) and fintech has fostered an entrepreneurial mindset among Cypriots (Elia, Margherita & Passiante, 2020).

DOI: 10.4324/9781003616108-7

However, despite this burgeoning entrepreneurial ecosystem, the availability of flexible workspaces in Cyprus has not kept pace with the rapid global development of coworking spaces.

In this chapter, we will delve into the case of MyOffice Cyprus, a coworking space company established by Panayiotis, a digital entrepreneur, to transform the perception and utilization of workspaces in Cyprus (Sussan & Acs, 2017). Despite the limited focus on entrepreneurship and technological innovation in his surroundings, he pursued a degree in computer science due to his passion for exploring new possibilities. Like many islanders, he watched as the world around him transformed through technology. But, unlike most, he saw beyond Cyprus's traditional career paths.

With a computer science degree in his pocket and experience working for multinational companies, Panayiotis had a front-row seat to the global digital revolution. Digital entrepreneurship encourages shifting from traditional business models to networked and integrated digital platform business models (Baranauskas & Raišienė, 2022; Komodromos, 2017; Reuschke, Clifton, & Fisher, 2021). Entrepreneurs can utilize platform-based innovation ecosystems to streamline the innovation process and cater to needs at both the invention and commercialization stages (Hsieh & Wu, 2019).

MyOffice was established to meet the increasing demand for flexible, community-focused workspaces tailored for freelancers, startups and remote workers. Through the strategic use of technology and a focus on customer needs, MyOffice swiftly gained prominence in the coworking industry of Cyprus, thereby playing a significant role in the country's evolving business landscape.

Contextual Background—The Spark of Inspiration

The Global Coworking Movement

Coworking emerged in the mid-2000s, driven by the increasing number of freelancers and entrepreneurs seeking alternatives to traditional office spaces' inflexible and often costly nature. Pioneers of coworking spaces envisioned them as collaborative environments where individuals and small businesses could share resources, knowledge and inspiration (Avdikos & Iliopoulou, 2019). Over time, coworking evolved from a niche offering into a mainstream solution for modern professionals, fueled by three major trends: the rise of the gig economy, the surge in remote work and the demand for flexible employment arrangements (Yacoub & Haefliger, 2022).

During his travels to cities like Athens, London and Berlin, Panayiotis discovered something that would change his life—and eventually, the face of business in Cyprus. He witnessed the magic of coworking spaces, where freelancers, startups and established companies shared not just office space, but ideas, energy and opportunities. "Why doesn't Cyprus have anything like this?", he wondered. The answer would lead him on an entrepreneurial journey to transform the island's work culture.

As Panayiotis returned home, he perceived Cyprus in a fresh light. The island was evolving—fintech startups were rising, digital nomads were uncovering its attractions and a new wave of entrepreneurs was emerging. However, many were working from home or in cafes, missing the collaborative energy he had experienced overseas. Before long, the workspace buzzed with excitement. Freelance designers teamed up with tech startups, digital nomads exchanged ideas with local business owners and international firms established a presence in Cyprus through virtual office solutions. MyOffice had transformed into precisely what Panayiotis envisioned—a hub for innovation and development.

Building the Dream

Based on industry research, the global coworking space market has been growing at an annual rate of approximately 20%. By 2024, there were more than 21,000 coworking spaces worldwide. The industry has established its role in supporting various business activities, including startup incubation, corporate innovation, freelancing and digital nomadism. Major coworking brands such as WeWork, Regus and Spaces have met this demand by creating networks of coworking spaces in cities worldwide.

Several factors have contributed to the widespread popularity of coworking spaces. Numerous studies suggest that this popularity is driven by factors such as urbanization, digital transformation, community and knowledge-sharing, flexible work environments and the rise of independent and remote work (Bouncken & Reuschl, 2016; Komodromos et al., 2024; Mariotti, Akhavan, & Rossi, 2021; Méndez-Ortega et al., 2023; Riratanaphong, 2021; Vogl & Micek, 2023).

Technological advances such as high-speed internet, cloud computing and collaboration tools have empowered workers to be productive from nearly any location.

Changing work preferences have led many professionals to favor flexible working arrangements, allowing them to manage their work-life balance effectively.

For startups and freelancers, coworking spaces offer cost-effectiveness by providing access to well-equipped offices without the high upfront costs of leasing traditional office space. By providing flexibility, affordability and a sense of community, coworking spaces have redefined how people approach work, fostering innovation and collaboration across various industries (Hsieh & Wu, 2019; Komodromos, 2017; Wall & Crowe, 2023).

Starting MyOffice wasn't easy. Panayiotis began with personal savings and small loans from friends and family like many entrepreneurs. He knocked on doors, pitched his vision and slowly built a network of believers who shared his dream of transforming Cyprus's work culture. The early days were challenging. Traditional businesses were skeptical of the coworking concept. "Why would anyone want to share an office?", they asked. But Panayiotis knew something they didn't—the future of work was changing, and Cyprus needed to change with it.

The Cypriot Business Environment

Cyprus has experienced notable changes in its business landscape in recent years. While it has been traditionally recognized for industries like tourism, real estate and shipping, the digital economy is now growing. Information and communication technology (ICT), fintech and renewable energy have emerged as significant sectors, attracting local entrepreneurs and international investors to the island. The government has actively supported entrepreneurship through tax incentives, startup grants and initiatives to strengthen the country's tech ecosystem.

By the early 2020s, despite technological advances, the Cypriot market had yet to embrace coworking spaces fully. Most available office spaces were traditional long-term leases, often too expensive and inflexible for freelancers and small businesses. As a result, many professionals worked from home, missing out on the collaborative energy and networking opportunities necessary for business growth. Additionally, Cypriot companies needed to be faster in adopting the flexible work models that had already become popular in major European markets.

The demand for coworking spaces grew as more entrepreneurs, startups and digital nomads began operating in Cyprus. This presented a unique opportunity for MyOffice to become a leader in a burgeoning market. MyOffice's mission was not only to provide flexible office space, but also to build a community that would foster collaboration, creativity and innovation. Its impact on the local business ecosystem became evident as it bridged a critical gap between the needs of modern professionals and the outdated office space solutions in Cyprus.

The Entrepreneur Behind MyOffice—More Than Just an Office

In recent years, digital entrepreneurship has become a driving force behind the transformation of various industries. It has revolutionized traditional business models, encouraged innovation and provided solutions to new social and economic challenges. Among the notable figures in this space is Panayiotis, a Cypriot entrepreneur whose journey led to the founding of MyOffice Cyprus. This digital enterprise transformed the workplace culture on the island. This chapter provides a detailed account of Panayiotis' entrepreneurial path, highlighting the motivation, funding strategies and challenges that paved the way for MyOffice to become a leading player in Cyprus' coworking industry in the following years.

MyOffice was designed to be more than just a place to work. Panayiotis envisioned a community hub where ideas could flourish and businesses could grow. He integrated smart technology throughout the space—from automated booking systems to virtual office solutions. But the real magic wasn't in the technology; it was in the connections being made.

Panayiotis' early career included working in various multinational firms, where he gained valuable experience in technology and business management. Although successful in the corporate world, Panayiotis felt a solid entrepreneurial drive to create something of his own. His interest in using technology to address social challenges led him to explore ideas that could benefit his community. While abroad, Panayiotis noticed the rise of coworking spaces in cities like Athens, London and Berlin. He was impressed by the flexibility, collaboration and sense of community these spaces offered. Upon returning to Cyprus, he realized that modern, flexible workspaces like those he had seen abroad were lacking despite the country's growth in fintech and information technology.

Finally, after recognizing a gap in the market, Panayiotis sought to create a coworking space that not only addressed the physical needs of modern professionals but also fostered a community-driven environment conducive to networking, collaboration and innovation. This focus on community became the cornerstone of MyOffice's business model, positioning it as not just a shared office space, but a hub for entrepreneurship.

MyOffice: The Business Model

Technology-Driven Solutions

MyOffice stands out by prioritizing the integration of technology into the workspace. The company utilizes intelligent workspaces, mobile apps and custom platforms to improve the customer experience. These technologies simplify tasks such as booking meeting rooms, managing memberships and accessing facilities remotely. This focus on digital integration aligns with global coworking trends, where technology is essential for flexibility and efficiency (Kyriakou et al., 2023).

Flexible Memberships and Revenue Streams

MyOffice provides flexible physical office space and offers adaptable membership plans. This allows professionals to choose workspace options based on their needs, including part-time desks, private offices and virtual office services. MyOffice is a highly versatile solution for a wide range of users. In addition to workspace options, MyOffice has diversified its revenue streams by hosting events, offering training workshops and forming strategic partnerships with other businesses. These additional services enable the company to engage with the entrepreneurial community beyond workspace rental, supporting professional development and networking opportunities for its members.

The Idea of the Digital Enterprise

MyOffice Cyprus originated when Panayiotis identified a gap in the Cypriot business landscape. At the time, the island's economy heavily relied on industries such as tourism, shipping and real estate, which mainly served large enterprises with traditional office setups. However, with the rise of digital entrepreneurship, the emergence of the gig economy and an increasing number of freelancers and startups,

Panayiotis saw an opportunity to introduce something new to the market. His vision was to establish a coworking space that offered physical workspaces and cultivated a community of innovators, freelancers and entrepreneurs who could collaborate and develop their businesses.

Panayiotis's digital enterprise aimed to address the need for more affordable, flexible and community-driven workspaces in Cyprus. Many freelancers and small startups needed help finding offices that met their needs without the burden of long-term leases and high upfront costs. As a result, many ended up working from home, missing out on the networking and collaborative opportunities that coworking spaces offered. Panayiotis envisioned MyOffice Cyprus as a solution to this problem. He aimed to create a coworking space that offered more than just desks and internet access. His vision was establishing a hub for innovation, professional development and collaboration. Through MyOffice, Panayiotis aimed to cultivate a culture of entrepreneurship and digital innovation that could compete on the global stage, ultimately helping to diversify the Cypriot economy.

Promoting Entrepreneurship in Cyprus

MyOffice's impact on entrepreneurship in Cyprus extends past providing office space. The company plays a crucial role in shaping the island's entrepreneurial ecosystem by nurturing a community of innovators, freelancers and startups. Regular events like networking sessions, workshops and mentoring programs create opportunities for members to learn from each other, form new partnerships and collaborate on projects. The emergence of coworking spaces like MyOffice aligns with the global trend of digital entrepreneurship, where businesses utilize digital platforms to innovate and commercialize products and services. In the case of MyOffice, the digital tools and services integrated into the workspace enable professionals to manage their work seamlessly and collaborate more efficiently, contributing to an environment where entrepreneurship can thrive.

Addressing the Social Challenge: A Need for Collaboration and Innovation

MyOffice, like many businesses, encountered significant challenges during the COVID-19 pandemic. When the COVID-19 pandemic hit, many thought it would end coworking. But Panayiotis saw it differently.

While others retreated, MyOffice adapted. They introduced virtual services, enhanced their digital offerings and created new ways for their community to stay connected even when physically apart. This adaptability proved crucial. As the world emerged from lockdowns, the demand for flexible workspaces soared. Remote work had become mainstream, and MyOffice was perfectly positioned to meet the needs of this new reality.

With lockdowns and restrictions on in-person gatherings, the demand for physical office space dropped dramatically. However, the pandemic also emphasized the importance of flexible work arrangements. Coworking spaces such as MyOffice proved resilient by offering virtual services and adapting to remote work trends. By providing digital tools and virtual office memberships, MyOffice maintained its relevance during global uncertainty. Panayiotis aimed to tackle a critical social challenge with his digital enterprise: the need for a modern, flexible approach to work. With its long leases and rigid structure, the traditional office model needed to be more suitable for the growing number of digital entrepreneurs, freelancers and startups in Cyprus. Additionally, Cyprus had to be faster in adopting the remote work models already gaining popularity in other European markets. This delay created a gap between the needs of the emerging tech sector and the available infrastructure.

Panayiotis realized that he could close this gap by creating a coworking space tailored to the needs of digital entrepreneurs and small businesses. He believed a collaborative workspace would provide the physical resources businesses needed and promote a sense of community that could inspire innovation and growth. Panayiotis aimed to foster entrepreneurship and viewed MyOffice as a means to drive digital transformation throughout the island. He believed that by offering a platform for digital professionals to connect and collaborate, MyOffice could assist Cyprus in competing in the global digital economy.

Funding the Digital Enterprise

Establishing a digital enterprise such as MyOffice was a challenging endeavor, and one of Panayiotis' main obstacles was securing the required funding. In the initial phases of the business, Panayiotis heavily relied on personal savings and small loans from friends and family to launch the venture. Additionally, he accessed various government grants and startup incentives to promote entrepreneurship and innovation in Cyprus. Panayiotis used his funds to reach out to potential investors interested in supporting local innovation. These investors recognized the potential in coworking spaces. They provided the initial capital needed to secure a physical location and invest in the necessary technology to make MyOffice a fully functioning digital hub.

Panayiotis' ability to build relationships with investors and business partners was crucial to MyOffice's early success. Through his network, he brought on board key collaborators who shared his vision for transforming the Cypriot work environment. This allowed him to expand the business and provide additional services like virtual offices, meeting rooms and event spaces.

Growth and Success of MyOffice: Looking to the Future

MyOffice rapidly became popular, drawing in diverse professionals, including freelancers, digital nomads, small startups and established companies. Its success was driven by Panayiotis' emphasis on offering not just physical workspaces, but also a supportive community where professionals could collaborate, share ideas and expand their businesses.

As MyOffice's business expanded, the company began offering a more comprehensive range of services to cater to a diverse clientele. In addition to coworking spaces, MyOffice started providing virtual offices, enabling businesses to have a professional presence in Cyprus without needing a physical office. This was especially appealing to international companies seeking to enter the Cypriot market.

One key factor in MyOffice's growth was its ability to adapt to the changing needs of the modern workforce. With the rise of remote work, Panayiotis recognized the importance of providing flexible solutions catering to local and international clients. MyOffice currently has a presence in two locations in Nicosia, but Panayiotis envisions expanding into multiple locations across the island. He also aims to introduce new services such as networking events, workshops and mentorship programs for entrepreneurs. But most importantly, MyOffice has shown that it's possible to create meaningful change with vision, determination and a commitment to the community. The company has helped position Cyprus as a modern, dynamic business destination, ready to compete in the global digital economy.

The Journey Continues

The story of Panayiotis and MyOffice Cyprus demonstrates the power of digital entrepreneurship and its impact on local economies. By identifying a market gap and using technology to provide innovative solutions, Panayiotis created a successful business that not only met the needs of modern professionals but also contributed to the growth of the Cypriot economy. Through MyOffice, Panayiotis has helped shape a new workplace culture in Cyprus that is flexible, collaborative and driven by innovation.

Despite the challenges, MyOffice plans to continue growing. Expansion to other cities in Cyprus, including Limassol and Larnaca, is on the horizon. Additionally, the company plans to introduce new services such as mentorship programs, accelerator initiatives and more comprehensive virtual office solutions. The company aims to remain a leader in the Cypriot coworking industry by continually adapting to the needs of its members and embracing the latest trends in digital entrepreneurship. Papnayiotis and the MyOffice journey emphasize the significance of adaptability, community-building and digital transformation in achieving success for contemporary businesses. By offering an alternative space for how Cypriots work, it has contributed to the island's transformation, fostering a brighter, more interconnected and innovative future for upcoming generations.

References

Avdikos, V. & Iliopoulou, E. (2019). Community-led coworking spaces: From co-location to collaboration and collectivization. In: Gill, R., Pratt, A.C., Virani, T.E. (eds), *Creative Hubs in Question. Dynamics of Virtual Work*. Palgrave Macmillan, Cham. https://doi.org/10.1007/978-3-030-10653-9_6.

Bara nauskas, G. & Raišienė, A. (2022). Transition to digital entrepreneurship with a quest of sustainability: Development of a new conceptual framework. *Sustainability*, *14*(3), 1104. https://doi.org/10.3390/su14031104

Bouncken, R. & Reuschl, A. (2016). Coworking-spaces: How a phenomenon of the sharing economy builds a novel trend for the workplace and for entrepreneurship. *Review of Managerial Science*, *12*, 317–334. https://doi.org/10.1007/s11846-016-0215-y.

Elia, G., Margherita, A., & Passiante, G. (2020). Digital entrepreneurship ecosystem: How digital technologies and collective intelligence are reshaping the entrepreneurial process. *Technological Forecasting and Social Change*, *150*, 119791. https://doi.org/10.1016/j.techfore.2019.119791

Hsieh, Y. & Wu, Y. (2019). Entrepreneurship through the platform strategy in the digital era: Insights and research opportunities. *Computers in Human Behavior*, *95*, 315–323. https://doi.org/10.1016/j.chb.2018.03.033.

Huang, H., Liu, Y., Liang, Y., Vargas, D., & Zhang, L. (2020). Spatial perspectives on coworking spaces and related practices in Beijing. *Built Environment*, *46*, 40–54. https://doi.org/10.2148/benv.46.1.40.

Kinsman, N., Marris, N., & Oakman, J. (2023). The impact of coworking spaces on workers' performance, mental and physical health: A scoping review. *Work*, *77*(1), 61–75. https://doi.org/10.3233/WOR-220353

Komodromos, M. (2017). Social networking: How small organisations are using Facebook and Twitter in engaging customers. *International Journal of Technology Marketing*, *12*(2), 142–150. https://doi.org/10.1504/IJTMKT.2017.083370

Komodromos, M., Harkiolakis, T., Khoshtaria T., & Vassiliou, M. (2024). Adoption of digital technology and investigation of the impact in the marketing industry for marketing communication professionals: The case study of Cyprus and Greece. *International Journal of Technology Enhanced Learning*, *16*(2), 173–191.

Kyriakou, C., Papaioannou, T., & Komodromos, M. (2023). Online criticism and cancel culture in digital marketing: A case study of audience perceptions of brand cancellation. *International Journal of Technology Enhanced Learning*, *15*(4), 2023, 412–427.

Mariotti, I., Akhavan, M., & Rossi, F. (2021). The preferred location of coworking spaces in Italy: An empirical investigation in urban and peripheral areas. *European Planning Studies*, *31*, 467–489. https://doi.org/10.1080/09654313.2021.1895080.

Méndez-Ortega, C., Smit, M., & Micek, G. (2023). Location patterns and drivers of coworking spaces in European Regions. Tijdschrift voor Economische en Sociale Geografie. https://doi.org/10.1111/tesg.12603.

Reuschke, D., Clifton, N., & Fisher, M. (2021). Coworking in homes – Mitigating the tensions of the freelance economy. *Geoforum*, *119*, 122–132. https://doi.org/10.1016/J.GEOFORUM.2021.01.005.

Riratanaphong, C. (2021). Factors influencing user satisfaction: Case studies of ten coworking spaces. Proceedings of International Structural Engineering and Construction. https://doi.org/10.14455/isec.2021.8(1).fam-04.

Robelski, S., Keller, H., Harth, V., & Mache, S. (2019). Coworking spaces: The better home office? A psychosocial and health-related perspective on an emerging work environment. *International Journal of Environmental Research and Public Health*, *16*, 1–22. https://doi.org/10.3390/ijerph16132379.

Sussan, F. & Acs, Z. (2017). The digital entrepreneurial ecosystem. *Small Business Economics*, *49*, 55–73. https://doi.org/10.2139/ssrn.2918535.

Vogl, T. & Micek, G. (2023). Work-leisure concepts and tourism: Studying the relationship between hybrid coworking spaces and the accommodation industry in peripheral areas of Germany. *World Leisure Journal*, *65*, 276–298. https://doi.org/10.1080/16078055.2023.2208081

Wall, S. & Crowe, P. (2023). Identifying the social, urban, and environmental co-benefits of coworking spaces in Irish towns. *Sustainability*, *16*(1), 175. https://doi.org/10.3390/su16010175

Yacoub, G. & Haefliger, S. (2022). Coworking spaces and collaborative practices. *Organization*, *31*(1), 87–114. https://doi.org/10.1177/13505084221074037

8 Jordan: Ethnic Fashion and Sustainability in the MENA Region

The Case of Sanaa Mohammad in Jordan

Tatiana Harkiolakis, Baker Ahmad Alserhan and Ruba Nizar Qahoush

A recent fashion area that emphasizes environmental responsibility, cultural traditions and ethical production practices is ethnic sustainable fashion, which involves integrating sustainable production practices with traditional cultural elements (Ojukwu & Tariq, 2020). This movement has gained traction as a response to the negative impacts of fast fashion, in which the cultural significance of traditional garment-making methods is overlooked, and laborers are often exploited (Bureekhampun & Maneepun, 2021). Ethnic sustainable fashion respects the environment while preserving cultural identities, establishing a harmonious blend between traditional craftsmanship and using ecologically friendly materials (Almalki & Tawfiq, 2023).

Although the combination of ethnic and sustainable fashion is growing in popularity, consumer uptake of these problems remains challenging in some areas of the world, such as the MENA region, where consumers exhibit high levels of consumption and preference for luxury products (Alserhan et al., 2014; Munir, 2020). Entrepreneurs launching sustainable fashion ventures also face long-term challenges in marketing their products and sustaining their business (Alsayed, 2024; Saxena et al., 2024). This chapter aims to explore these challenges through the case of Sanaa Mohammad, a solo entrepreneur who launched an ethnic sustainable fashion enterprise in Jordan selling clothes produced from upcycled denim.

DOI: 10.4324/9781003616108-8

Sustainable Fashion

The fashion industry contributes to a staggering amount of waste and pollution worldwide, contributing to 20% of water pollution worldwide and 10% of global carbon emissions (European Parliament, 2020). Waste during a garment's lifecycle occurs during the production process, such as chemical residues and the waste of leftover materials, as well as after its purchase by the consumer when garments are thrown away (Al-Shareef & Alharbi, 2023). Fast fashion, in which new styles are produced quickly and sold at meager prices, contributes significantly to this waste. Each year, 92 million tons of textiles are disposed of, while less than 1% of clothing waste is recycled (Members' Research Service, 2022).

The rise of sustainable fashion indicates a growing trend around addressing the social and environmental consequences of the traditional fashion industry, combatting these consequences through innovative approaches such as the circular economy, where waste is reduced and ethical production practices are promoted (Hou et al., 2024). This evolving sector is notable for responding to the growing environmental and social degradation caused by fast fashion, including ecological degradation, poor labor conditions and consumerism's inherent wastefulness (Bealby-Wright & Leurent, 2024). Consumers and activists have compelled the fashion industry to reassess its production processes and embrace transparency, circularity, eco-friendly materials and fair labor policies as sustainability issues receive greater global attention (Dana et al., 2024).

Central to sustainable fashion is the concept of the circular economy, which emphasizes the reuse, recycling and upcycling of materials to minimize waste and maximize the lifecycle of each garment (Almalki & Tawfiq, 2023). The process of transforming discarded clothing into new, high-value products while fostering creativity and reducing textile waste, known as upcycling, has emerged as a growing trend in this area. By changing unwanted products or waste fabric into new items without using any new raw materials, upcycling has become a critical component of the circular economy. New garments with equal or added value compared to that of the originals can be created (Quagrainie, 2023). By fostering creativity in design, this practice reduces waste while encouraging new innovative methods of garment production. Upcycled fashion products are often unique and durable and carry their narratives, enabling consumers to engage with sustainability meaningfully (Saepudin et al., 2023).

Upcycling involves various techniques that allow individuals and designers to reimagine and recreate garments (Kim, 2024). Standard methods include sewing, dyeing, embroidery and patchwork (de Aguiar Hugo et al., 2021). For instance, an old T-shirt can be cut and sewn into a tote bag, while denim jeans can be restructured into stylish jackets. These techniques transform items that might otherwise be discarded into unique fashion statements, encouraging individuals to personalize their wardrobes and express their creativity (Quagrainie, 2023).

The upcycling process typically begins with sourcing raw materials, which can come from surplus stock, second-hand shops or donations. Designers assess the character and history of the materials, identifying unique textures, patterns and imperfections that can be celebrated in the new design (Gautam, 2024). This approach reduces waste and helps conserve valuable resources such as water and energy that would be expended in creating new garments. One of the fundamental pillars of upcycling is using eco-friendly materials (Rehman et al., 2024). These materials include textiles such as organic cotton, recycled polyester and bamboo fibers, significantly reducing the environmental impact of clothing production. Sustainable materials not only conserve natural resources but also offer unique benefits in terms of comfort and durability, aligning with consumer demand for responsible products (de Aguiar Hugo et al., 2021).

However, transitioning to a circular model has challenges, including economic disparities, accessibility issues and systemic industry practices that often prioritize profit over sustainability (Gautam, 2024). Despite growing consumer awareness and demand for sustainable fashion, accepting upcycled clothes presents a challenge. Consumers of fashion, particularly luxury fashion, tend to see garments as a way to express wealth and status, which contradicts the concept of used garments or leftover fabric scraps (Elmanadily & El-Deeb, 2022). Many consumers are also deterred by the high price of upcycled clothes, which reflects the intense time and labor investments made into each handmade garment compared to mass-produced fast fashion products (Munir, 2020).

Ethnic Sustainable Fashion

Ethnic dress reflects the lifestyle and aesthetic styles of an ethnic group, which has been defined as a cultural group with a shared history and traditions (Kaya & Romanescu, 2022). Ethnic fashions continue to thrive in the face of globalization and international cultural influences because consumers connect emotionally to representations of their ethnic groups (Singh, 2024). These fashion items can include clothing, jewelry and accessories. Technological innovations drive a wave of fashion with ethnic elements produced through modern design and production processes. Some scholars see technological innovations and modernized designs as crucial to preserving ethnic fashions, which risk losing their appeal to younger consumers in the face of globalized fashion trends (Deng et al., 2023).

Research is emerging regarding the sustainable production of ethnic fashion garments (Deng et al., 2023). Traditional ethnic fashions are usually inherently in line with sustainability principles, centered around being handmade, high-quality, durable and meant for long-term wear, in contrast to the consume-and-throw model of fast fashion (Almalki & Tawfiq, 2023). Many traditional garment-making techniques utilize natural materials, such as natural dyes that do not contribute to water pollution, and zero-waste approaches to production (Al-Shareef & Alharbi, 2023).

Contemporary designers increasingly collaborate with artisans and communities to incorporate traditional techniques into modern designs, thus promoting sustainability while honoring cultural heritage (Chairani et al., 2024). By reviving these practices, they not only preserve historical artistry but also support local economies and foster a sense of community identity (Deng et al., 2023). Such techniques also facilitate the preservation of cultural heritage, enabling communities to maintain their identities while adapting to contemporary fashion demands (Tang et al., 2023).

Cultural influences in fashion extend beyond aesthetics to include deeper narratives and symbolism (Kaya & Romanescu, 2022). Each cultural tradition possesses a unique tapestry of stories and beliefs that can be woven into contemporary fashion. Incorporating indigenous patterns and motifs into modern designs creates a dialogue that honors cultural heritage while promoting a sustainable future (Almalki & Tawfiq, 2023). Designers prioritizing traditional craftsmanship and ethical practices are paving the way for a movement emphasizing sustainability and cultural diversity in fashion (Ojukwu & Tariq, 2020).

Entrepreneurs in the ethnic sustainable fashion sector often emerge from within their communities, leveraging cultural knowledge and networks (Singh, 2024). These entrepreneurs play a pivotal role in preserving traditional crafts and promoting sustainable practices. Their ventures contribute to economic development and community cohesion (Lyon et al., 2023). The success of these enterprises often hinges on the ability to balance cultural authenticity with market demands. Entrepreneurs must navigate the complexities of maintaining traditional aesthetics while appealing to contemporary consumers. This balance requires innovation, adaptability and a deep understanding of cultural heritage and market trends (Alblowi et al., 2021).

Entrepreneurs in ethnic sustainable fashion face several challenges, including limited access to sustainable materials, lack of infrastructure for eco-friendly production and market competition (Alshibani et al., 2024). Additionally, the absence of clear regulations and standards for sustainable fashion can lead to inconsistencies and consumer skepticism (Puglia et al., 2024). Despite these challenges, there are significant opportunities for growth. The rich cultural heritage associated with ethnic fashion provides a unique market differentiation platform. Collaborations between designers, artisans and organizations can foster innovation and support the development of a sustainable fashion ecosystem (Bureekhampun & Maneepun, 2021).

However, penetrating international markets remains a significant challenge, as these markets often prioritize cost-effectiveness over sustainability (Singh, 2024). Competing against mass-produced garments necessitates a focus on quality and the effective communication of the value proposition of sustainable fashion products. Furthermore, promoting traditional craftsmanship through social media and digital platforms allows a broader audience to appreciate the rich heritage embodied in ethnic wear (Chairani et al., 2024). There is a burgeoning interest in integrating traditional handmade techniques with modern design, which creates unique, high-quality products that stand out in a market dominated by mass-produced items (Alblowi et al., 2021). These products carry cultural heritage stories and foster emotional connections with consumers, adding intangible value. This fusion of old and new will likely shape the aesthetics and narrative of future fashion collections, leading to a revival of artisan communities and providing them with sustainable livelihoods (Bureekhampun & Maneepun, 2021).

Consumer behavior also plays a critical role in the challenges faced by ethnic sustainable fashion (Khan et al., 2023). While many consumers desire sustainable products, there is a tendency toward impulse buying, which undermines sustainable practices (Saepudin et al.,

2023). Companies must not only promote sustainable consumption but also work to foster sustainable habits among consumers. These efforts include setting standards for ethical production and encouraging customers to make informed choices that align with sustainability goals (Alsayed, 2024).

Ethnic Sustainable Fashion in the MENA Region

Among MENA consumers, there is a growing interest in understanding the role of ethnic fashion in promoting sustainability (Alblowi et al., 2021). Ethnic fashion offers a unique avenue for promoting sustainability by incorporating locally sourced materials and preserving cultural heritage. Cultural values and ethical considerations have significantly shaped consumer interest in sustainable fashion. In MENA markets, cultural sustainability plays a pivotal role in shaping consumer preferences (Alblowi et al., 2021). Ethical consumerism is still emerging in the region, with consumers showing a growing awareness of the environmental and social implications of their fashion choices (Munir, 2020). In the MENA region, this movement is emerging, influenced by traditional practices and modern consumer awareness. While the concept of sustainability is not new to the area—given historical practices of resourcefulness—the formal adoption of sustainable fashion is still in its nascent stages (Almalki & Tawfiq, 2023).

However, the transition from awareness to actual consumer behavior remains a challenge. Marketing in the MENA region, particularly in Islamic markets, involves various cultural, religious and legal considerations (Alserhan et al., 2022). Studies have shown that women consumers in this region pay careful attention to the quality of items purchased (Alserhan et al., 2015), which sets the bar high for sustainable fashion items to reach the quality of traditionally produced fashion items.

Consumers in the MENA region often face the limited availability of sustainable products and higher costs associated with ethically produced fashion items (Elmanadily & El-Deeb, 2022). Price sensitivity is another factor influencing consumer behavior. Sustainable fashion often costs more due to ethical production methods and quality materials (Saepudin et al., 2023). This can be a barrier to adoption in markets where consumers are price-conscious. Brands must find ways to make sustainable fashion accessible without compromising ethical standards (Saepudin et al., 2023). The Arab Fashion Council

(AFC) has been instrumental in promoting sustainability among consumers. In 2018, the AFC launched the "AFC Green Label" initiative to encourage designers to adopt eco-friendly practices and materials, aligning with the United Nations Sustainable Development Goals (Arab Fashion Council, n.d.). This initiative reflects a growing institutional support for sustainable fashion in the region.

A significant trend in sustainable fashion is the integration of cultural elements into product offerings to appeal to specific consumer groups (Alblowi et al., 2021). MENA consumers exhibit a strong preference for fashion that reflects their cultural heritage. Designers increasingly incorporate traditional elements into modern designs, appealing to a sense of identity and pride. For instance, traditional embroidery and patterns in contemporary clothing have been well-received among consumers seeking a connection to their roots (Modhy, 2023). Including traditional motifs and designs can enhance the perceived value of sustainable fashion products among MENA consumers (Alshibani et al., 2024).

Brands increasingly leverage cultural elements to establish brand differentiation and connect with niche markets (Kaya & Romanescu, 2022). However, integrating cultural aspects into sustainable fashion presents challenges. Designers must balance cultural authenticity with sustainable practices, which can be resource-intensive and require innovation (Khan et al., 2023). Challenges also remain in fully integrating sustainable practices into the fashion industry within MENA markets. These include limited access to sustainable materials, a lack of infrastructure for eco-friendly production and a market still developing an appreciation for sustainable products (Alshibani et al., 2024). Additionally, the absence of clear regulations and standards for sustainable fashion can lead to inconsistencies and consumer skepticism (Manshoven & Van Opstal, 2022).

One key barrier is the lack of consumer education about the benefits of sustainable fashion (Munir, 2020). Many consumers are unaware of the environmental impacts of their purchasing decisions and may prioritize aesthetic appeal or brand prestige over sustainability credentials. Additionally, cultural perceptions and economic factors, such as the higher costs of sustainable clothing, further limit the adoption of sustainable fashion in these markets (Elmanadily & El-Deeb, 2022). Despite these challenges, there are growth opportunities. The rich cultural heritage of the MENA region provides a unique platform for designers to create distinctive, sustainable fashion that resonates with consumers. Collaborations between designers, artisans and organizations can foster innovation and support the development of a sustainable fashion ecosystem (Almalki & Tawfiq, 2023).

Method

An embedded single-case study represents a methodological approach focused on examining multiple dimensions within a single case, typically an organization (Yin, 2018). This approach enables comprehensive data analysis and within-case investigation, providing a basis for juxtaposing findings with those from comparable cases in existing literature (Eisenhardt, 2020). By facilitating the exploration of subunits within larger cases, this design supports data collection from secondary or archival sources (Yin, 2018).

Qualitative research methods offer distinct advantages, particularly their capacity for in-depth exploration anchored in a conceptual framework (Yin, 2018) and facilitating an analysis of participants' experiences (Sanders Muhammad, 2020). Case studies are mainly valuable for addressing 'how' and 'what' questions concerning contemporary phenomena in natural contexts (Halkias et al., 2023; Halkias & Neubert, 2020). This approach is especially relevant when researchers have minimal control over external variables (Halkias et al., 2022). Single-case studies focus on examining and analyzing units within a case, yielding a deeper understanding of the subject. Data collection in single-case research, particularly in entrepreneurial studies, can be effectively executed through archival records and observations, providing additional insights into the case (Henry & Foss, 2015).

Archival research constitutes a systematic approach to knowledge inquiry involving searching, analyzing and drawing inferences from archival data (Corti & Thompson, 2004). Such archives are essential for understanding organizational practices (Perkins et al., 2010), identifying emerging issues and enhancing the reliability of findings (Corti & Thompson, 2004). Researchers can gather data by observing individual events or sequences over extended periods, and document collection serves as a valuable data source in case study research.

The distinction between embedded and non-embedded units of analysis lies in their contextual differences. While embedded units operate within a similar, or potentially identical, environment, "stand-alone" units do not. In case studies focusing on a single unit of analysis, the boundary between a unit of analysis and its embedded context may become less distinct (Yin, 2018). In a single embedded case study or a single-case study with embedded units, the 'case' can refer to an event, entity or context beyond a single individual (Yin, 2018, p. 29). This single embedded case study, which examines Sanaa Mohammad's enterprise based in Jordan, is a holistic, individual inquiry approach tailored to a single-case study design. The study focuses on the case narrative and its alignment with theoretical propositions (Yin, 2018).

The Case Study

Background of the Protagonist: An Entrepreneur's Journey

Sanaa Mohammad's foray into the fashion business began during the COVID-19 pandemic. Having studied languages at university, Sanaa had always drawn sketches of dresses and other ready-to-wear garments as a hobby. During the period's frequent lockdowns, Sanaa filled her time at home by taking online courses about the business of fashion and design. She began taking her ideas from sketches to finalized designs, buying a sewing machine to make prototypes of her designs at home, despite struggling with the space requirements for sewing machines at home and the distance from actual instructors. Sanaa kept perfecting her designs and teaching herself sewing techniques, producing clothes for her family members to wear. Her family quickly saw her potential and encouraged her to take more courses in the business of fashion.

After the period of lockdowns ended, Sanaa realized that she wanted her passion for fashion design to go beyond a fun hobby and define her career journey. She enrolled in a garment design school in Jordan. There, Sanaa learned more about pattern-making and stitching, as well as about managing a fashion business and understanding functions such as imports and exports. During a course on business development, Sanaa learned about how the fashion industry is one of the world's biggest polluters and perpetuates unethical practices such as child labor. Sanaa considered these dangers in light of the drastic changes to society and everyday life after the pandemic, where environmental conservation was becoming a growing concern for individuals and businesses. It was then that Sanaa decided to begin her journey into sustainable fashion.

For her final project, Sanaa put together a mood board about what she wanted to pursue in the future. Her mood board centered around upcycling and recycling, specifically denim, and transferring old denim fabric to a new, completely different garment. Denim is notoriously challenging to decompose in nature, and its processing involves heavy chemicals and color dyes that can cause significant water pollution. These processes are also cost- and labor-intensive. Upcycling denim scraps, abundantly available in factories, is more sustainable and significantly reduces the time and labor needed to produce a new garment.

Researching on her own the extent of fabric scraps in factories in Jordan, she discovered that 20% of fabric from garment-making is left over per factory. These fabric scraps are either thrown away into landfills or burned, contributing to air pollution from fossil fuels. Sanaa also noticed that Jordan has abundant second-hand clothing stores that throw away unsold garments, further contributing to a cycle of pollution and consumption.

Gathering fabric scraps from factories, Sanaa wanted to combine them into a new garment connected to Jordan's culture and history. She was inspired by Jordan's historical mosaics, which reminded her that "small pieces can be combined and create the whole picture" (S. Mohammad, personal communication, October 22, 2024). Broken mosaic pieces are combined into completely different formations to make works of art. Sanaa decided to take scraps of garments destined for landfills and combine them to create something new—pulling small pieces together to make a significant impact, one garment at a time.

Sanaa's designs incorporated these ethnic fashion traditions through symmetrical and asymmetrical designs of combined fabric scraps, which she developed from sketches and finalized through a partnership with a local fabric factory. Sanaa's work also took inspiration from traditional quilting techniques, such as seamlessly combining fabric scraps into one functional item. The resulting garments were unique and well-structured, yet usable for everyone and suitable for every occasion. Her first target customers were consumers who cared about sustainability and sought out the value of artistic, handmade, recycled garments that took time and consideration to produce. In 2023, Sanaa entered her resulting garments into a fashion design competition. Her capsule collection won first place for the Spring/Summer collection, giving her vast exposure and launching her dream into a fully sustainable ethnic fashion enterprise.

Background Information on the Product: Ethnic Fashion Meets Sustainability

Sanaa's designs use ethnic fashion motifs and techniques, following the tradition of Jordanian mosaics and traditional patchwork techniques. Her designs are inspired by the natural environment and seasons and the designs and colors seen on animals, insects and buildings. Her design process begins with collecting individual elements to combine into a larger design, using sketches and mood boards to help her determine the aesthetics of each garment and how to incorporate the elements.

Sanna incorporates the ideals of sustainability by considering how each piece will serve the community and the broader ecosystem. Each piece is designed to be worn in everyday life to maximize its use. Sanaa's enterprise follows the belief that circular business models are the key to a more sustainable future for people, businesses and the planet. Upcycling fabric scraps allows her enterprise to create garments that do not jeopardize the environment or contribute to the alarming amounts of waste and pollution generated by the fashion industry. Her circular production processes also allow her and her partners to maintain a social conscience through fair labor practices, knowing their work will benefit the wider community. Additionally, she continues refining her designs and materials, working on making her existing garments more sustainable and incorporating more pre-existing fabric.

The Protagonist's Challenges: Business Growth and Marketing Sustainable Fashion as a Solo Entrepreneur

Sanaa's prize for winning the competition was meant to be international exposure and the chance to participate in international fashion shows. Due to the outbreak of the war in Gaza in the fall of 2023, however, the competition had to suspend its activities in the Gulf region. Sanaa applied for support from institutions that offered funding and mentorship to entrepreneurs, including fashion schools and non-profits, but received no responses. This situation left Sanaa to find a way to grow her business and market her products.

This challenge loomed for her in an industry where personal connections and access can determine an entrepreneur's success.

These factors are amplified in a country like Jordan, where a small circle of industry insiders can easily exclude a budding entrepreneur they see as a threat. The Jordanian public did not regard the idea of pre-used or sustainable garments. Additionally, small collections of one-of-a-kind, expensive, time- and labor-intensive pieces can be difficult to market in the face of competition from fast fashion companies that produce thousands of garments for a single collection. On top of everything, Sanaa had to juggle her enterprise with her 9-to-5 job as an escalation specialist at a startup, leaving her with no time to pursue further in-depth training in the business of fashion. Fashion courses at universities and training institutes in Jordan are also expensive and have limited options for financial support.

Not to be deterred, Sanaa completed her collection of 40 designs independently. In the aftermath of the competition, she was invited by a local university to showcase her garments and talk about her entrepreneurial journey to the students at the university's fashion school. Nonetheless, she faced the question of how to market her finished products. She considered hiring a marketing company or a partner to handle the business side of her enterprise. Still, those she consulted wanted a large payment or a large share of her enterprise.

Instead, Sanaa turned to social media and leveraged fashion communication and marketing techniques, sending work samples to influencers and launching campaigns on platforms like Instagram. Digital marketing efforts are crucial to reaching younger and tech-savvy consumers (Komodromos et al., 2024), with Instagram being one of the key social media platforms embraced by young consumers (Harkiolakis & Diamantaki, 2022). She combined these techniques with on-ground efforts, such as participating in fashion, jewelry and handicraft bazaars. The owner of an annual craft bazaar at a large hotel, in particular, saw potential in her designs and gave her a table at the bazaar for free. The owner invited Sanaa to another bazaar in Riyadh, but she rejected the offer due to the high travel costs. Despite this obstacle, Sanaa's efforts paid off, with her two collections selling out almost immediately.

Marketing upcycled garments made from fabric scraps and fabric from used clothes to the Jordanian public presents challenges. From time to time, Sanaa faces concerns from her customers about the hygiene of wearing used fabrics. At her partner factory, Sanaa ensured that the used scraps of denim were put through a rigorous sanitization process and a fabric analysis for allergy testing. Only high-quality pieces of denim made from 100% organic cotton are chosen to be made into new garments. The resulting clothes are of high quality so as to not resemble upcycling. Sanaa also filmed the process and broke it down into short videos to show her customers who expressed hygiene concerns. As the circular business model became more familiar to the Jordanian public, more and more consumers began opening up to sustainable, circular fashion.

The mix of on-ground and digital efforts was the start of Sanaa's long-term marketing and communications strategy, utilizing Instagram as a space to market her products to tech-savvy and environmentally and socially conscious consumers. She refined her target audience to be women aged 18 to 45 with high incomes who prefer statement pieces, love to try new things, prize uniqueness in their fashion items and look for powerful yet feminine and elegant items. These characteristics have helped Sanaa carve out a unique brand identity.

Epilogue

Women entrepreneurs tend to face unique challenges in launching their enterprises (George-Ufot & Halkias, 2021; Halkias & Caracatsanis, 2016; Halkias et al., 2011, 2016; Howard et al., 2019; Ojong et al., 2021; Polideras et al., 2016;). Sanaa was lucky not to face significant gendered barriers in beginning her enterprise and aims to inspire more women to pursue careers sustainably. However, Sanaa initially struggled with juggling managing a business and her creative outputs. Creative entrepreneurs face the challenge of designing and developing products and services and handling other business functions such as marketing, manufacturing and finances. Although Sanaa received much support and knowledge from her online courses, the garment design school she attended and her partners in the business, she saw a need for more long-term mentoring initiatives in Jordan to help nurture creative entrepreneurs through the business development process, from forming an initial business plan to marketing finalized products.

Being a solo entrepreneur also proved challenging when dealing with legal issues, such as defining the intellectual property for her designs, which incorporate traditional ethnic motifs. The process required endless document-signing procedures, and Sanaa would have had to create her commercial records. Ethnic fashion motifs can complicate this process further, as the copyright on traditional designs is often unclear and contested. These processes are expensive, and Sanaa quickly realized she would also need legal support or consultation as she saw other designers copying her exact designs.

When launching and sustaining her enterprise, financial support was also a key concern for Sanaa. Without available government or institutional financial support, she received financial support from her family and generous vacation time from her employer. She also received financial support from the factory owner she worked with during her entry into the competition. The factory owner supported manufacturing the final product in exchange for a small percentage of the profits. Nevertheless, finances remain a concern for her enterprise's long-term growth. More governmental and institutional financial support and training for entrepreneurs in Jordan could support more talented young minds in launching innovative enterprises that can give back to the country's economic growth and productivity (Aljaouni et al., 2020). Reskilling and upskilling initiatives are also valuable for teaching entrepreneurs about utilizing technologies to launch and sustain their businesses (Diaz & Halkias, 2021; Dana et al., 2024; Diaz et al., 2022; Halkias et al., 2023).

Conclusion

The future of ethnic sustainable fashion is poised to be transformative, driven by a growing demand for environmentally friendly materials and practices within the fashion industry (Ojukwu & Tariq, 2020). As consumers increasingly seek transparency and ethical standards from brands, traditional textiles and garment-making techniques are gaining prominence due to their sustainable attributes and cultural significance (Almalki & Tawfiq, 2023). This trend is about aesthetic appeal and fostering a deeper appreciation for the artistry and craftsmanship involved in traditional textile production, which serves to preserve diverse cultural heritages. This chapter explored the journey of one ethnic sustainable fashion enterprise based in Jordan to understand the challenges and opportunities in this burgeoning fashion industry sector.

With an eye toward the future, Sanaa plans to launch a website for her brand to boost sales eventually. She is working on the legal processes to copyright her designs to prevent their theft by other designers. Her plans included making the processing phase of the garments easier and quicker; given the high amount of labor, time and money put into each garment in previous collections, the sales price of each final garment was high. Making her garments more affordable can open up her creations to a broader target audience. Sanaa is also exploring incorporating a variety of fabrics into her designs, beyond denim. She aims to one day market her business to the international market, particularly other Gulf nations and global fashion centers such as Italy.

Although our study strived for the greatest methodological and conceptual rigor, limitations of our current study include the choice of the embedded single-case study method, the geographical focus on a single nation in the MENA region and the conceptual focus on upcycling. Future research can employ qualitative, semi-structured interviews to understand the experiences of multiple ethnic sustainable fashion entrepreneurs. Quantitative research can also be conducted to understand the relationship between relevant variables in this sector, such as the relationship between cultural background and consumers' willingness to purchase ethnic sustainable fashion products. Future research can also explore the MENA region regarding sustainable ethnic fashion trends and compare this region to others worldwide where ethnic fashion is prominent, such as China and India. Finally, scholars can also explore different ethnic sustainable fashion techniques, such as natural dyeing processes, recycled fabrics, zero-waste production processes and ethnic motifs in sustainable garments.

Acknowledgments

The authors thank Ms. Sanaa Mohammad for participating in an in-depth interview to provide information for this case study.

References

Alblowi, R., Henninger, C. E., Parker-Strak, R., & Blazquez, M. (2021). The influence of culture on the sustainable entrepreneur: An investigation into fashion entrepreneurs in Saudi Arabia. In M. Á. Gardetti & S. S. Muthu (Eds.), *Handloom sustainability and culture: Entrepreneurship, culture and luxury* (pp. 71–86). Springer Singapore. https://doi.org/10.1007/978-981-16-5967-6_4

Aljaouni, N. W., Alserhan, B., Gleason, K., & Zeqiri, J. (2020). Financial literacy programs and youth entrepreneurial attitudes: Some insights from the Jordanian community. *Journal of Enterprising Communities: People and Places in the Global Economy*, *14*(5), 787–810. https://doi.org/10.1108/JEC-07-2020-0128

Almalki, D. K. & Tawfiq, W. A. (2023). Implementation of a sustainable apparel design framework for felted women's garments made of local wool. *Fashion Practice*, *15*(3), 401–423. https://doi.org/10.1080/17569370.2023.2186033

Alsayed, R. (2024). *Consumers' acceptance to buy and dispose of recycling textile products* [Master's thesis, The American University in Cairo]. AUC Knowledge Fountain. https://fount.aucegypt.edu/etds/2227

Alserhan, B. A., Bataineh, M. K., Halkias, D., & Komodromos, M. (2014). Measuring luxury brand consumption and female consumers' religiosity in the UAE. *Journal of Developmental Entrepreneurship*, *19*(02), Article 1450009. https://doi.org/10.1142/S1084946714500095

Alserhan, B. A., Halkias, D., Boulanouar, A. W., Dayan, M., & Alserhan, O. A. (2015). Expressing herself through brands: The Arab woman's perspective. *Journal of Research in Marketing and Entrepreneurship*, *17*(1), 36–53. https://doi.org/10.1108/JRME-09-2014-0024

Alserhan, B. A., Ramadani, V., Zeqiri, J., & Dana, L. P. (2022). *Strategic Islamic marketing*. Springer.

Al-Shareef, D. A. & Alharbi, M. M. (2023). Sustainable fashion design of Al-Sadu fabric by using zero waste. *International Design Journal*, *13*(3), 71–82. https://doi.org/10.21608/idj.2023.296260

Alshibani, S. M., Shabir, S., & Albishri, N. (2024). Women entrepreneur's perspective towards sustainable entrepreneurship in the apparel sector of Saudi Arabia. *Sustainability*, *16*(19), Article 8636. https://doi.org/10.3390/su16198636

Arab Fashion Council. (n.d.). *AFC Green Label and sustainability*. Retrieved November 8, 2024, from https://arabfashioncouncil.com/afc-green-label/

Bealby-Wright, O. & Leurent, H. (2024). Shifting the needle: Can we build the next generation of consumer activism and advocacy for sustainable fashion? In M. Charter, B. Pan, & S. Black (Eds.), *Accelerating sustainability in fashion, clothing and textiles* (pp. 203–215). Routledge.

Bureekhampun, S. & Maneepun, C. (2021). Eco-Friendly and community sustainable textile fabric dyeing methods from Thai buffalo manure: From pasture to fashion designer. *SAGE Open*, *11*(4), 1–13. https://doi.org/10.1177/21582440211058201

Chairani, R., Muftiadi, A., Herawaty, T., & Rizal, M. (2024). Consumer buying decisions for ethnic fashion: Investigating the roles of digital marketing, brand image, and product innovation. *Journal of System and Management Sciences*, *14*(11), 462–474. https://doi.org/10.33168/JSMS.2024.1125

Corti, L. & Thompson, P. (2004). Secondary analysis of archived data. In C. Seal, G. Gobo, J. F. Gubrium, & D. Silverman (Eds.), *Qualitative research practice* (pp. 297–311). Sage.

Dana, L. P., Boardman, R., Salamzadeh, A., Pereira, V., & Brandstrup, M. (Eds.). (2024). *Fashion and environmental sustainability: Entrepreneurship, innovation and technology*. De Gruyter.

Dana, L. P., Crocco, E., Culasso, F., & Giacosa, E. (2024). Mapping the field of digital entrepreneurship: A topic modeling approach. *International Entrepreneurship and Management Journal, 20*(2), 1011–1045. https://doi.org/10.1007/s11365-023-00926-6

de Aguiar Hugo, A., de Nadae, J., & da Silva Lima, R. (2021). Can fashion be circular? A literature review on circular economy barriers, drivers, and practices in the fashion industry's productive chain. *Sustainability, 13*(21), Article 12246. https://doi.org/10.3390/su132112246

Deng, M., Liu, Y., & Chen, L. (2023). AI-driven innovation in ethnic clothing design: An intersection of machine learning and cultural heritage. *Electronic Research Archive, 31*(9), 5793–5814. https://doi.org/10.3934/era.2023295

Diaz, J. & Halkias, D. (2021). Reskilling and upskilling 4IR leaders in business schools through an innovative executive education ecosystem: An integrative literature review. *SSRN Electronic Journal.* http://dx.doi.org/10.2139/ssrn.3897059

Diaz, J., Halkias, D., & Thurman, P. W. (2022). *The innovative management education ecosystem: Reskilling and upskilling the future workforce.* Routledge.

Eisenhardt, K. M. (2020). Theorizing from cases: A commentary. In L. Eden, B. B. Nielsen, & A. Verbeke (Eds.), *Research methods in international business* (pp. 221–227). Palgrave Macmillan.

Elmanadily, D. & El-Deeb, S. (2022). A study on consumers' purchase intentions and willingness to pay more towards eco-fashion clothes. *South Asian Journal of Management, 29*(3), 161–190. https://sajm-amdisa.org/images/stories/pdf/sajmvol.%2029.3-abstract.pdf

European Parliament. (2020, January 29). *The impact of textile production and waste on the environment (infographics).* Retrieved September 12, 2024, from www.europarl.europa.eu/topics/en/article/20201208STO93327/the-impact-of-textile-production-and-waste-on-the-environment-infographics

Gautam, R. (2024). The narrative of circular economy and sustainability – A critical analysis of fashion industry. Circular Economy and Sustainability. Advanced online publication. https://doi.org/10.1007/s43615-024-00417-y

George-Ufot, D. & Halkias, D. (2021). Challenges of women micro-entrepreneurs in the Niger Delta Region of Nigeria for business survival: A narrative inquiry. *ISM Journal of International Business, 4*(1), 1–11.

Halkias, D. & Caracatsanis, S. M. (2016). The evolution of researching female immigrant entrepreneurship: A commentary. In D. Halkias, P. Thurman, S. Caracatsanis, & N. Harkiolakis (Eds.), *Female immigrant entrepreneurs* (pp. 3–8). Gower.

Halkias, D., Esposito, M., Harkiolakis, T., Diaz, J., & Ikpogu, N. M. (2023). Digital entrepreneurship and disruptive innovation in the Greek maritime industry: the case of Harbor Lab. In V. Ramadani, S. Kjosev, & B. S. Sergi (Eds.), *Entrepreneurship development in the Balkans: Perspective from diverse contexts* (pp. 131–150). Emerald Publishing.

Halkias, D. & Neubert, M. (2020). Extension of theory in leadership and management studies using the multiple case study design. *International Leadership Journal*, *12*(2), 48–73. http://dx.doi.org/10.2139/ssrn.3586256

Halkias, D., Neubert, M., Thurman, P. W., & Harkiolakis, N. (2022). *The multiple case study design: Methodology and application for management education*. Routledge.

Halkias, D., Nwajiuba, C., Harkiolakis, N., & Caracatsanis, S. M. (2011). Challenges facing women entrepreneurs in Nigeria. *Management Research Review*, *34*(2), 221–235. https://doi.org/10.1108/01409171111102821

Halkias, D., Thurman, P., Caracatsanis, S., & Harkiolakis, N. (2016). *Female immigrant entrepreneurs: The economic and social impact of a global phenomenon*. CRC Press.

Harkiolakis, T. & Diamantaki, K. (2022). The professional practices of travel journalists on Instagram: A generic qualitative study. *International Journal of Technology Enhanced Learning*, *14*(4), 382–401. https://doi.org/10.1504/IJTEL.2022.125854

Henry, C. & Foss, L. (2015). Case sensitive? A review of the literature on the use of case method in entrepreneurship research. *International Journal of Entrepreneurial Behaviour & Research*, *21*(3), 389–409. https://doi.org/10.1108/IJEBR-03-2014-0054

Hou, J., Wang, X., Yao, S. Y., & Aris, A. (2024). Sustainable fashion design: A review and perspective. *International Journal of Art and Design*, *8*(2/SI), 95–104. https://doi.org/10.24191/ijad.v8i2/SI.3576

Howard, D. L., Halkias, D., & Dean, H. (2019). Women's entrepreneurial leadership practices and enterprise longevity: An integrative literature review. *SSRN Electronic Journal.* http://dx.doi.org/10.2139/ssrn.3355595

Kaya, Ö. & Romanescu, L. S. C. (2022). Representation of ethnic diversity in the collections of fashion brands–2005–2020. *Învățământ, Cercetare, Creație*, *8*(1), 191–199. www.ceeol.com/search/article-detail?id=1051934

Khan, S. J., Badghish, S., Kaur, P., Sharma, R., & Dhir, A. (2023). What motivates the purchasing of green apparel products? A systematic review and future research agenda. *Business Strategy and the Environment*, *32*(7), 4183–4201. https://doi.org/10.1002/bse.3360

Kim, Y. (2024). Proximity dimensions in making fashion circular: A systematic literature review and implications for cities and regions. *Cities*, *148*, Article 104870. https://doi.org/10.1016/j.cities.2024.104870

Komodromos, M., Harkiolakis, T., Khoshtaria, T., & Vassiliou, M. (2024). Adoption of digital technology and investigation of the impact in the marketing industry for marketing communication professionals: The case study of Cyprus and Greece. *International Journal of Technology Enhanced Learning*, *16*(2), 173–191. https://doi.org/10.1504/IJTEL.2024.137650

Lyon, F., Elf, P., Owen, R., & Werner, A. (2023). Finance and funding for upscaling sustainable fashion. In M. Charter, B. Pan, & S. Black (Eds.),

Accelerating sustainability in fashion, clothing and textiles (pp. 105–115). Routledge.

Manshoven, S. & Van Opstal, W. (2022). The carrot or the stick? Stakeholder support for mandatory regulations towards a circular fashion system. *Sustainability, 14*(22), Article 14671. https://doi.org/10.3390/su142214671

Members' Research Service. (2022, May 4). *Textiles and the environment.* European Parliamentary Research Service. https://epthinktank.eu/2022/05/04/textiles-and-the-environment/

Modhy, K. (2023, July 6). *Are Saudi Arabia's luxury consumers looking for sustainable, ethical, and ethnic options?* Fast Company. https://fastcompanyme.com/impact/are-saudi-arabias-luxury-consumers-looking-for-sustainable-ethical-and-ethnic-options/

Munir, S. (2020). Eco-fashion adoption in the UAE: Understanding consumer barriers and motivational factors. *Fashion Practice, 12*(3), 371–393. https://doi.org/10.1080/17569370.2020.1777729

Ojong, N., Simba, A., & Dana, L. P. (2021). Female entrepreneurship in Africa: A review, trends, and future research directions. *Journal of Business Research, 132*, 233–248. https://doi.org/10.1016/j.jbusres.2021.04.032

Ojukwu, O. A. & Tariq, T. (2020). *Rethinking sustainability in the fashion industry through indigenous culture* [Master's thesis, Politecnico Milano]. POLITesi. https://hdl.handle.net/10589/167484

Perkins, L. N., Nightingale, D., Valerdi, R., & Rifkin, S. (2010). Organizational assessment models for enterprise transformation. *INCOSE International Symposium, 20*(1), 809–823. https://doi.org/10.1002/j.2334-5837.2010.tb01106.x

Polideras, K., Abadir, S., Robotis, P., & Halkias, D. (2016). Canada: The Greek female entrepreneurs of Montreal. In D. Halkias, P. Thurman, S. Caracatsanis, & N. Harkiolakis (Eds.), *Female immigrant entrepreneurs* (pp. 197–206). Gower.

Puglia, M., Parker, L., Clube, R. K., Demirel, P., & Aurisicchio, M. (2024). The circular policy canvas: Mapping the European Union's policies for a sustainable fashion textiles industry. *Resources, Conservation and Recycling, 204*, Article 107459. https://doi.org/10.1016/j.resconrec.2024.107459

Quagrainie, F. A. (2023). An environmental sustainability model for Ghanaian clothing: A fashion cycle approach. In L.-P. Dana, R. Boardman, A. Salamzadeh, V. Pereira, & M. Brandstrup (Eds.), *Fashion and Environmental Sustainability* (pp. 261–278). De Gruyter.

Rehman, M., Petrillo, A., Ortíz-Barrios, M., Forcina, A., Baffo, I., & De Felice, F. (2024). Sustainable fashion: Mapping waste streams and life cycle management. *Journal of Cleaner Production, 444*, Article 141279. https://doi.org/10.1016/j.jclepro.2024.141279

Saepudin, D., Shojaei, A. S., Barbosa, B., & Pedrosa, I. (2023). Intention to purchase eco-friendly handcrafted fashion products for gifting and personal use: A comparison of national and foreign consumers. *Behavioral Sciences*, *13*(2), Article 171. https://doi.org/10.3390/bs13020171

Sanders Muhammad, R. (2020). African American women managers' experiences in predominantly black work environments: A multiple case study. *International Journal of Teaching and Case Studies*, *11*(2), 133–156. https://doi.org/10.1504/IJTCS.2020.109722

Saxena, A. P., Kumar, P., Rathor, H., Shrivastav, H., & Soni, S. (2024). Fashion for ethnic wear: A case study of Manyavar Fashion. *Lloyd Business Review*, *3*(1), 1–14. https://doi.org/10.56595/lbr.v3i1.16

Singh, S. (2024). Ethnic fashion designers, entrepreneurs and family businesses: An African marketing perspective. *Journal of Family Business Management*, *14*(3), 663–671. https://doi.org/10.1108/JFBM-09-2023-0156

Tang, D., Koh, P. C. L., & Wong, S. K. (2023). A study of female consumer behaviour and consumption experience on fashion products with ethnic elements in China. *Academic Journal of Business & Management*, *5*(25), 21–27. https://doi.org/10.25236/AJBM.2023.052503

United Nations in Jordan. (2023, June 14). *Meet the winner of Khayt fashion design competition (Spring/Summer) collection*. https://jordan.un.org/en/238255-meet-winner-khayt-fashion-design-competition-springsummer-collection

Yin, R. K. (2018). *Case study research and applications: Design and methods* (6th ed.). Sage.

Index

Note: The acronyms "MENA" and "UAE" refer to "Middle East and North Africa" and "United Arab Emirates" respectively.

AFC (Arab Fashion Council) 86–87
affordability 8, 20, 43, 50–51, 62, 72
African banking 51–56, 65–66
alternative packaging, for wine 33–34
Arab Fashion Council (AFC) 86–87
artificial intelligence (AI), in India 39–47
Aziz, Nour 31–33, 36

B2B (business-to-business) 18, 25, 26, 27, 47, 61
B2C (business-to-consumer) 18, 24, 25, 26
Bamba, Régis 50, 51, 57, 59
Bourgi, Hassan 50, 57, 59
branding 32, 34, 35, 45, 65, 71, 86, 87, 93, 94
business development 93
business models 1–2, 3, 26, 56, 60, 64, 70, 73, 74, 91, 93
business-to-business (B2B) 18, 25, 26, 27, 47, 61
business-to-consumer (B2C) 18, 24, 25, 26

canned wine 32, 35, 36
CardioMate 41, 42, 44
Ceylan 18, 22, 23–24, 25, 26, 27
Chakraverty, Abhilash 41, 42, 44
collaboration 21, 63, 85, 88; government 64; and MyOffice Cyprus 71, 72, 73, 74, 75–76
composting 18, 20, 21, 22, 23, 24–25
consumer behavior 18, 19, 22, 85–86
consumer education 22, 87–88
COVID-19 pandemic 18, 19, 34–35, 40, 75–76, 89; and SaludAbierta 10, 11, 12, 15
coworking spaces 69, 70–72, 73, 74, 75–76, 77, 78
culture 3–4, 81, 84, 87; workplace 69–78
Cypriot business environment 72–73
Cyprus, workplace culture in 69–78

denim 81, 83, 90, 92–93, 95
developing economies: entrepreneurship in 39–41; and financial inclusion 51
development 1, 15–16, 64, 65; business 93; of coworking spaces 70, 71; economic 3, 52, 54, 64, 85; entrepreneurial 27, 28; professional 74, 75; sustainable 4, 87, 88
Dhalla, Pritam 39, 41, 42, 43–44
diabetes 10, 15
diagnosis, and treatment 42–43
diagnostics, artificial intelligence (AI) in 39–47
digital enterprise 73, 74–75, 76–77

digital entrepreneurship: in Cyprus 69, 70, 73, 74–75, 78; and disruptive innovation 1–4
digital technologies 1, 2–3, 56; in health 39–41
disruptive innovation: and digital entrepreneurship 1–4; ecosystems of 2–3; and Larkai Healthcare 47; The Waste Lab as 26; in wine industry 31–37
Djamo 50–51, 57, 58–66

economic development 3, 52, 54, 64, 85
economic growth 1, 2, 3, 4, 54, 59, 64, 94
ecosystem, building an 63
e-healthcare 9
entrepreneurial development 27, 28
entrepreneurial journey 19, 57, 71, 92
entrepreneurship: in Cyprus 75; in developing economies 39–41
ethnic dress 83–84
ethnic fashion 84, 85, 86, 90, 93–94, 95; *see also* ethnic sustainable fashion
ethnic sustainable fashion 81, 83–86, 91, 94, 95; in MENA region 86–88

finances 44, 58, 62, 93, 94; *see also* financial support
financial inclusion, in Ivory Coast 50–66
financial services 52, 53, 55, 56, 64, 65; and expanding product offerings 62–63; leveraging technology to transform 57–59
financial support 92, 94; *see also* finances
financial technology 53, 54, 55, 57–59, 62
Fintech 51–56, 57, 59–62, 63, 64, 65, 69
food waste: global 19–22; in UAE 18, 19, 22–23
Francophone Africa 51, 52, 54–55, 56; and Djamo 59–62, 64, 65; and Hassan Bourgi 57

geographical expansion 63, 66
global aspirations 45
global coworking movement 70–71
global coworking space market 71
global food waste 19–22
government collaboration 64

healthcare access: in India 39–47; in Peru 10–11
healthcare industry 7, 8, 39–40
healthcare technology 7, 12, 15, 40, 41; *see also* patient-monitoring technology
Hussein, Lara 18, 19, 23–24, 25, 26–27

India, artificial intelligence (AI) in 39–47
innovation 1–2, 75–76
international markets 35, 44, 85, 95
investor confidence 26–27
Ivory Coast, financial inclusion in 50–66

Jordan, ethnic sustainable fashion in 81–95

Komodromos, Panayiotis 73–74, 74–75, 75–76, 76–77, 78

Larkai Healthcare 39, 41, 42; and sustainability 46, 47
local aspirations 45

Marin, Ana 6–8, 13, 14
market penetration 63
marketing 26, 32, 81, 86, 92, 93
medical diagnostics, artificial intelligence (AI) in 39–47
MENA region, sustainability in 82, 83, 84, 85, 86, 87, 90, 91
methodology 88–89, 95

Middle East and North Africa region, sustainability in 82, 83, 84, 85, 86, 87, 90, 91
Mohammad, Sanaa 81, 89–90, 91, 92–94, 95
MyOffice Cyprus 70, 73, 74–75, 78

pandemic *see* COVID-19 pandemic
partnerships 12, 45, 74, 75, 90; and financial inclusion 56, 58, 63–64, 66; and food waste 25, 26, 27, 28
patient-monitoring technology 41, 42–43, 44, 46, 47
payment infrastructure 51, 53, 55, 60
personal finance super app 61–62
Peru, healthcare access in 6–16
policy advocacy 64
product offerings 55, 62–63, 65, 87
professional development 74, 75
protagonist's challenges 91–93
protagonist's dilemma 6–8, 36, 45

recycling 21, 23, 24, 33, 46, 82, 83, 90, 95
regional entrepreneurial ecosystems 1–2, 3

Salud Group 6, 7, 8–9, 11–12, 13, 14, 15
SaludAbierta 6, 7, 8, 9, 12–14, 15, 16
social impact 46–47
solo entrepreneur 81, 91–93
Spain, wine industry in 32, 36
sustainability: and ethnic fashion 91; and Larkai Healthcare 46, 47; in MENA region 82, 83, 84, 85, 86, 87, 90, 91; in UAE 22–23, 24, 28
sustainable development 4, 87, 88
sustainable fashion 82–83, 89, 94, 95; ethnic 83–88; marketing of 91–93
sustainable practices 22, 85–86, 87
sustainable products 85–86, 87

technology: artificial intelligence (AI) 39–47; and coworking 71, 72, 73, 74, 77, 78; digital 1, 2–3, 39–41, 56; financial 53, 54, 55, 57–59, 62; healthcare 7, 12, 15, 40, 41; innovation in 22, 70, 84; patient-monitoring 41, 42–43, 44, 46, 47
treatment, and diagnosis 42–43

UAE 18–28; sustainability in 22–23, 24, 28
upcycling 82, 83, 90, 91, 93, 95

value proposition 13, 15, 26, 27, 65, 85

Waste Lab, The 18, 19, 23–26, 26–27
websites 35, 94
Wine in a Can: company history and profile 34–35; market for 33–34; and market share 36–37; protagonist 31–33, 36
wine industry, in Spain 32, 36
wine packaging 33–34
workplace culture, in Cyprus 73, 78
WREN 41, 42–43, 44, 46, 47

For Product Safety Concerns and Information please contact our EU representative GPSR@taylorandfrancis.com Taylor & Francis Verlag GmbH, Kaufingerstraße 24, 80331 München, Germany

Printed and bound by CPI Group (UK) Ltd, Croydon, CR0 4YY
20/07/2026
02171554-0001